ROUTLEDGE LIBRARY EDITIONS:
LIBRARY AND INFORMATION SCIENCE

Volume 33

EMERGING PATTERNS OF COLLECTION DEVELOPMENT IN EXPANDING RESOURCE SHARING, ELECTRONIC INFORMATION AND NETWORK ENVIRONMENT

EMERGING PATTERNS OF COLLECTION DEVELOPMENT IN EXPANDING RESOURCE SHARING, ELECTRONIC INFORMATION AND NETWORK ENVIRONMENT

Edited by
SUL H. LEE

LONDON AND NEW YORK

First published in 1996 by The Haworth Press, Inc.

This edition first published in 2020
by Routledge
2 Park Square, Milton Park, Abingdon, Oxon OX14 4RN

and by Routledge
52 Vanderbilt Avenue, New York, NY 10017

Routledge is an imprint of the Taylor & Francis Group, an informa business

© 1996 The Haworth Press, Inc.

All rights reserved. No part of this book may be reprinted or reproduced or utilised in any form or by any electronic, mechanical, or other means, now known or hereafter invented, including photocopying and recording, or in any information storage or retrieval system, without permission in writing from the publishers.

Trademark notice: Product or corporate names may be trademarks or registered trademarks, and are used only for identification and explanation without intent to infringe.

British Library Cataloguing in Publication Data
A catalogue record for this book is available from the British Library

ISBN: 978-0-367-34616-4 (Set)
ISBN: 978-0-429-34352-0 (Set) (ebk)
ISBN: 978-0-367-40993-7 (Volume 33) (hbk)
ISBN: 978-0-367-41004-9 (Volume 33) (pbk)
ISBN: 978-0-367-81043-6 (Volume 33) (ebk)

Publisher's Note
The publisher has gone to great lengths to ensure the quality of this reprint but points out that some imperfections in the original copies may be apparent.

Disclaimer
The publisher has made every effort to trace copyright holders and would welcome correspondence from those they have been unable to trace.

Emerging Patterns of Collection Development in Expanding Resource Sharing, Electronic Information and Network Environment

Sul H. Lee
Editor

The Haworth Press, Inc.
New York • London

Emerging Patterns of Collection Development in Expanding Resource Sharing, Electronic Information and Network Environment has also been published as *Journal of Library Administration* Volume 24, Numbers 1/2, 1996.

© 1996 by The Haworth Press, Inc. All rights reserved. No part of this work may be reproduced or utilized in any form or by any means, electronic or mechanical, including photocopying, microfilm and recording, or by any information storage and retrieval system, without permission in writing from the publisher. Printed in the United States of America.

The development, preparation, and publication of this work has been undertaken with great care. However, the publisher, employees, editors, and agents of The Haworth Press and all imprints of The Haworth Press, Inc., including The Haworth Medical Press and Pharmaceutical Products Press, are not responsible for any errors contained herein or for consequences that may ensue from use of materials or information contained in this work. Opinions expressed by the author(s) are not necessarily those of The Haworth Press, Inc.

Cover design by Monica L. Seifert

The Haworth Press, Inc., 10 Alice Street, Binghamton, NY 13904-1580 USA

Library of Congress Cataloging-in-Publication Data

Emerging patterns of collection development in expanding resource sharing, electronic information and network environment / Sul H. Lee, editor.
    p. cm.
  Published also as v. 24, no. 1/2, 1996 of Journal of library administration.
  Includes bibliographical references and index.
  ISBN 0-7890-0033-4 (alk. paper)
  1. Collection development (Libraries)–United States–Congresses. 2. Library cooperation–United States–Congresses. 3. Academic libraries–Collection development–United States–Congresses. I. Lee, Sul H.
Z687.2.U6E44 1997
025.2′1–dc21
                                                      96-52926
                                                          CIP

For Melissa

Emerging Patterns of Collection Development in Expanding Resource Sharing, Electronic Information and Network Environment

CONTENTS

Introduction *Sul H. Lee*	1
Library Collections and Distance Information: New Models of Collection Development for the 21st Century *Harold Billings*	3
Library Collections at Century's End: Lessons from American Express *Genevieve S. Owens*	19
Designing Serial Collections for the 21st Century *Charles Hamaker*	35
Will Electronic Information Finally Result in Real Resource Sharing? *Frederick C. Lynden*	47

Friends or Predators: Evaluating Academic Periodicals' Price Histories as a Means of Making Subscription Decisions
    Anthony W. Ferguson
    Kathleen Kehoe
	73

Collecting, Sharing, and Networking: The Role
and Responsibilities of a National Library 87
William J. Sittig

Emerging Patterns of Partnership in Collection
Development: A Subscription Vendor's Perspective 103
Kit Kennedy

New Partners for Collection Development 113
Rebecca T. Lenzini

Index 125

Introduction

On March 7th and 8th, 1996, the University of Oklahoma Libraries and the University of Oklahoma Foundation sponsored "Emerging Patterns of Collection Development in Expanding Resource Sharing, Electronic Information and Network Environment." This conference was a continuation of previous conference presentations and discussions on important collection development and networking issues facing the library communities. This volume presents the papers delivered at the conference in the hope that librarians, students and other interested people will continue the investigations and discussions of these critical issues.

Mr. Harold Billings, Director, University Libraries at the University of Texas at Austin, develops a thoughtful presentation on the need for new collection development policies to reflect the environment in which libraries function. He notes that the continued strength of paper publishing and expanding digital sources requires libraries to think and act differently. Genevieve Owens, Program Manager for Information Resources Selection at Bucknell University, uses the American Express Company to explore the current and future role of libraries. Through the concepts of co-branding, brand extension and market segmentation, Ms. Owens provides comparative strategies for libraries.

Mr. Charles Hamaker, Assistant Dean for Collection Development at Louisiana State University, presents results from his continuing study of serial costs and collection development activities at LSU. He adds to his study on serial costs, suggests a new foundation on which to analyze serial needs, and looks to document delivery to meet the information demands of the academy. Mr. Frederick Lynden, Associate University Librarian for Technical Services at Brown University, investigates the aspects of electronic information as he considers their impact on resource sharing. In his conclusion he provides ten recommendations to improve resource sharing during the transitional period from paper to electronic format.

Mr. Anthony Ferguson, Associate University Librarian, and Ms. Kathleen Kehoe, Reference and Collection Development Librarian, at Columbia University, present a study of "friendly" and "predatory" periodicals. In their paper they suggest a number of actions libraries should consider in responding to the predators. William Sittig adds the perspective of national libraries to the discussion of economic and technical forces influencing libraries. He provides an overview of selected national libraries and then focuses on the important activities of the Library of Congress.

Ms. Kit Kennedy, Director of Academic Sales for Readmore Academic Services, gives an enlightening view of partnerships. From her perspective as a vendor, she provides interesting insight into the relationship of vendors and libraries. The last paper, by Ms. Rebecca T. Lenzini, President of CARL Corporation, provides a discussion of the changing roles of collection developers, models of information access and delivery and trends in information access and delivery.

The conference facilitated wonderful discussion among the presenters and participants. Perhaps the greatest success of such a meeting is this interaction. I hope the presentation of these papers in this volume will continue the dialogue and development of models for our use.

I wish to acknowledge the work of Mr. Don Hudson who, as conference coordinator, made this event a success. I would also like to thank Ms. Melanie Davidson and Mr. Wilbur Stolt for their help in the creation of this volume.

Sul H. Lee

Library Collections and Distance Information: New Models of Collection Development for the 21st Century

Harold Billings

A discussion of library collections, distance information, and emergent models of collection development by which information resources will be managed in the next century can be highlighted by several unarguable trends.

- If there is anyone who believes print-on-paper is dying they have not been reading publishing statistics.
- The ability of libraries to maintain acquisitions programs that keep up with the ongoing pace of paper-based publishing continues to diminish.
- As libraries continue to constrict their purchases towards their most basic needs, conventional wisdom would suggest that library collections are all beginning to look alike.

Recent research by Anna Perrault confirms this increasing homogeneity of academic library acquisitions and collections.[1] She notes

---

Harold Billings is Director, University Libraries at The University of Texas at Austin, Austin, TX.

[Haworth co-indexing entry note]: "Library Collections and Distance Information: New Models of Collection Development for the 21st Century." Billings, Harold. Co-published simultaneously in *Journal of Library Administration* (The Haworth Press, Inc.) Vol. 24, No. 1/2, 1996, pp. 3-17; and: *Emerging Patterns of Collection Development in Expanding Resource Sharing, Electronic Information and Network Environment* (ed: Sul H. Lee) The Haworth Press, Inc., 1996, pp. 3-17. Single or multiple copies of this article are available for a fee from The Haworth Document Delivery Service [1-800-342-9678, 9:00 a.m. - 5:00 p.m. (EST). E-mail address: getinfo@haworth.com].

that her findings support the Mellon report that suggests a "narrowing" of access to scholarly information, a concern that research libraries will look "more and more alike over time," and a resulting "decline in the richness of collections overall, not merely a decline in the range of holdings of any one library."[2]

- At the same time that print-on-paper publishing flourishes, the growth of distance information continues at an exponential pace. By this I mean the expansion of interlibrary services in all its variations, document delivery in its many manifestations, as well as the creation and distribution of information objects coruscating from a digital forge.

A major task for libraries in coming years will be the addition to their collections of appropriate books and journals in paper-based format, the management of an increasing proportion of information that will become available in digital form, and the communal melding of these information streams into a common pool for the fishing of information.

Libraries must modify and update collection development policies and procedures to recognize that the local collection will evolve into one enhanced and extended by digital technologies and electronic information sources. Policies for managing—and sharing—national and global mega-collections will emerge from the construction of cooperative programs on a scale that far transcends concerns for building the local collection.

We should not be surprised that policies will be and, indeed, are already being established by those governing bodies that fund our libraries to move us towards collection development practices that may conflict with what we have always presumed would be local or cooperative collection development decisions.

It is important that new models of collection development emerge to equip libraries, and the larger library and information community, for the responsibilities they will bear for access to all forms of information in the next century.

This paper touches briefly on issues where library collections and distance information come together on a policy level and how these issues will shape the future.

CHARACTERISTICS OF THE NEW INFORMATION ENVIRONMENT

Let me describe briefly what I believe to be some of the characteristics of the new information environment. The changing nature of information is providing a dramatic impetus towards a reconsideration of issues that have always been basic to collection development. Both artifactual and digital information must be selected, organized, preserved and delivered from physical collections and electronic repositories. Both analog and digital formats will be delivered locally or to distant locations by carriers appropriate to the format.

Professor William A. Wulf of the University of Virginia–in a wonderful article entitled "Warning: Information Technology Will Transform the University"–has recently described the changing nature of universities and libraries: "Instead of a hoarder of containers, the library must either become the facilitator of retrieval and dissemination or be relegated to the role of a museum. If we project far enough into the future, it's not clear whether there is a distinction between the library and the book," he says.[3]

"The technology of the bibliographic citation," he continues, "pales by comparison with the hypertextual link: the ability to gain immediate access to the full referenced source and hence to browse through the context of the reference. It will take a long time to build the web and especially to incorporate the paper legacy, but the value of a seamless mesh will doom the discrete isolated volume."

To my mind, the greatest challenge in managing this wealth of collections and interwebbed information will be to find a means to merge the information sources–and the results of searching these sources–in order to provide the content that satisfies the information seeker whether it be textual information, hypertext, raw data, response-invoking semiotics such as art or music, or that grander thing whatever it may be that we call knowledge.

The answer to this challenge will represent a resolution of economic, technological, ideational, and philosophical matters that will transform the information environment. In order to better understand that information scene, and the collection policies required to shape it, it might be well to consider some of its physical and temporal characteristics.

Time and distance will remain in the genetic structure of the print-on-paper model. Distance information carried by a stream of digital pulses is characterized by transmutability, manipulability, and a dangerous fragility. We do not yet really understand how to secure the permanent retention of such information or how to establish policies to guarantee an appropriate assignment of responsibility for its preservation.

Distance and location are of little moment to any format until the information is required. Geography is virtually negligible in the digital information world. It may not yet be the case that distance is dead, but it is certainly dying. Time, on the other hand, is very much an issue in the currentness of some content, how quickly it can be accessed, and as a condition of the mind that strokes it.

Selection will continue to be the most important issue in the total process of information service. Identification of prospective scholarly resources has become simpler in many regards as bibliographic and indexing tools have improved. But selection will become more complicated as the information world itself continues to expand and as information objects grow increasingly more complex.

Delivery will remain the most difficult problem for paper-based services. While distance—as noted above—is becoming virtually a non-issue in many areas of library service, it continues to be a significant barrier in others. As distance information becomes more routine—that is, as all our libraries rely increasingly on remote access as well as on the collections we have at hand—a new set of collection-building consternations will confront us at every level of decision-making in the acquisitions process. These must be treated in our collection policies.

One of the major problems that must be addressed in the new information environment will be an appropriate choice for what will be the chief characteristic of the information object. Will it be print or will it be digital? Will it be both?

Will the digital version provide for such a richer mixture of content, of information searching and retrieval capabilities, of extended information linking and expansion of knowledge availability that a paper version will be redundant and an unnecessary expense? Or will a paper copy represent a necessity for any one of a number of quite justifiable reasons—ease of use for content access, convenience as a mobile information unit, as a useful back-up, or as a warm and fuzzy security blanket for the intellectual child in each of us?

This issue is not as simple as deciding whether to acquire a title in one format or another, whether to bind it or not, whether to discard it after a period of time in which it is perceived to be useful in a physical format regardless of whether a digital version exists or not, or whether the title has significance because of its format, quality of construction, or artifactual significance. The issue should be considered more holistically in terms of defining what the total requirements are for effective, efficient access to knowledge sources, on a title by title basis, on an object by object basis, or a construct by construct basis, within the organic information world.

What are the fiscal issues involved in these choices?

Collection development policies must include such considerations as these as they are modified to fit the circumstance of this strange and wonderful new world in which the information object itself may well be a compound of multimedia content, of both client and server software, and of self-referential cataloging data.

What are some of the other special issues and challenges that will affect collection development at that borderline of dynamic tension where the physical library collection and the digital world of compound information converge, separate, augment one another, and do battle?

First of all, we can be absolutely secure in our knowledge that library services will be required in the information future. Librarians will continue to build value for systems that connect information and its prospective users. Librarians will be the tool-shapers and the information guides, hunters and fishers in this new information ecology. Many will continue their work in those locations we have called libraries.

Anyone who enters an enormous warehouse of books, or a vast star space of digital knowledge which has not been thoroughly organized, will quickly have to seek a librarian to achieve any major degree of success in an information search. A library as a repository for physical collections, as a central bank of subject and information retrieval expertise, as a station from which information missions depart, will be just as important in the information future as it has been in the information past.

On a very practical basis, libraries must negotiate much of the complex contractual web that determines to which digital information a user has access. Individuals have been able to buy books and subscribe to journals. Without some affiliation with libraries how will individuals be able to gain access to certain electronic information that requires payment at the door, and which may not be available through a commercial information service, or available only at greater expense from a non-library source? The library as a cost-center middleman, using economies of scale in its payment for information access, and in chasing the dream of making information as freely available as possible, will continue in a digital world as in print. Libraries will impose more cost-recovery charges for information access than in the past, but it appears certain that the cost to all of information-units delivered will decline.

Librarians will be indispensable in the development of collection development policies whether they be at the local level, at the cooperatively managed mega-collection level, or within a reshaped information management framework driven by those who control the institutional funding that dictates what libraries will collect and how they will share resources with one another.

THE ESTABLISHMENT OF COLLECTION DEVELOPMENT POLICIES

Twenty-five years ago most of our libraries were just beginning to establish collection development policies to assist in the management of our acquisition programs. Over the years these policies have been massaged, revised, perhaps even laid aside and forgotten as the quickening of research has produced more information for printed library materials, and as flat or reduced budgets have negated our best-laid plans for acquisition programs.

For the most part, those collection policies initiated in the 1970s included selection criteria regarding the academic and research interests to be supported, the scope and level of intensity at which these subjects would be acquired, and information regarding the language, publication date, and the formats appropriate for acquisition.

With the advent of expanded cooperative resource-sharing programs in the 1980s, the application of policies based on organizational agreements and national perspectives grew more intensive. These programs utilized such mechanisms as the National Shelf List Measurement Project, the RLG Conspectus, and other descriptive and analytical methodologies established among institutions involved in library networking cooperatives to rationalize collection building responsibilities among the participants.

Collection policies, of course, had moved on to include matters relating to duplication, disposition, disaster plans, and preservation.

While granting the continuing importance of these long-standing guidelines for the development of collections appropriate to local institutional needs, or for collections joined to one another symbiotically through resource-sharing agreements, the development of the digital library begs the introduction of entirely new considerations into collection development policy statements as we look towards the twenty-first century.

New factors–the rapidly increasing availability of network-accessible information resources, the incorporation of digitization into numerous information activities, and the concept of managed information–have not surprisingly started to emerge as issues to be incorporated into our selection policies.

In the 1995 edition of her useful textbook on collection development, the late Elizabeth Futas notes that some areas of collection development discussion "have not yet appeared in any discernible number of policies. Among these areas are the collecting and archiving of electronic journals, the Internet and its relationship to collection building, cooperative efforts in collection development and preservation of materials. Why these areas have yet to show up is somewhat perplexing since the library profession is certainly concerned about their impact on collection growth and development."[4]

Happily, these issues are now beginning to receive attention in the literature. The so-called "mainstreaming" of the selection of Internet resources into the collection development process has been extremely well introduced in a recent article by Demas, McDonald and Lawrence of Cornell University, growing out of earlier work by Demas.[5]

"We believe," they say, "it is time for collection development librarians to focus intensively on the processes of collection development as applied to networked and other electronic resources."

Beyond that, as they point out, "Applying the principles of selection to Internet-accessible resources is but one part of a larger challenge: learning how to select among a wide variety of potential access mechanisms."

In my view, the recognition that the same information resources may be available in print, microform, CD-ROM, locally mounted magnetic tape files, or in digital representations via various retrieval tools on the Internet, is still just a beginning at determining how we can best relate this multiplicity of resources to one another so that the knowledge seeker can most easily find the content that is being sought whether it is in a local or remote collection or regardless of the digital format in which it is enwrapped.

Each of our institutions will be exploring the addition of a new vocabulary to our collection development policies. These will describe our intention at the local level to deal with the mix of physical and digital resources that we will "acquire," but we will be looking, increasingly I believe, at other issues still to be addressed in collection development policy for the twenty-first century information environment. These issues will exist at a macro level reflecting larger institutional, state, and national policy issues than just our typical local collection orientation.

"Historically a university has been a place," William Wulf writes. Scholars gathered where they could be safe, where there were other scholars with whom to converse, where there was access to scholarly materials, and in contemporary times, to scientific instruments and library collections. "Where the scholars assembled, the students followed," Wulf says.

He cites John Cardinal Newman's nineteenth-century essays on the university in which Newman says if he had to describe what a university was, he would draw his answer from its ancient designation as a Stadium Generale: "This description implies the assemblage of strangers from all parts in one spot."

To me, in cyberspace all roads lead to a digital Rome. Indeed, any road can lead anywhere and everywhere. No one need be a stranger to any place, and virtual assemblages at the desktop will soon be common. I am speaking, of course, of digital access and teleconferencing.

Wulf continues: "With powerful ubiquitous computing and networking, I believe that each of the university's functions can be distributed in space, and possibly in time. Remote scholarship is the direct analog of telecommuting in the business world, and every bit as appealing."

It is suggested that computing and networking provide for a learner-centered environment rather than the traditional teacher-centered environment that has been a characteristic of the university as place. It appears to me that in cyberspace any element of the scholarly process can be centric at any time, or at all points in place and time, whether it be the teacher, the student—or the library collection.

TOWARDS MANAGED INFORMATION

It is apparent that there is a growing trend at all levels of education to consider carefully what the new technologies can do to help distribute the scholarly process, not because of the immediately perceived virtues of how technology can improve the system, but rather because of fiscal, demographic and social pressures.

Fiscal constrictions in higher education are certainly urging a distributed responsibility among educational institutions for the provision of support for distance education and for life-long learning. Teachers and students both must share their scholarly experience in the same company as the informational materials—the library collections—that must be readily available to them. Distance information will be a fundamental resource for distance learning. It is small wonder that there is such a strong swell of interest these days in digital libraries.

The forces at work at the macro level that will surely promote easy digital access to information of all kinds may well relegate our local collection development policies to a secondary status. These overriding forces will at once affect our local acquisitions programs as well as the resource-sharing activities through which we will increasingly provide access to information based on trans-institutional policies and directives.

It is clear to me that we are being steered by our funding bodies towards managed information programs, and our information acquisitions programs and collection development policies will increasingly reflect the influences of this pressure. I do not necessarily mean to criticize this tactic, but it is one that I believe should be more widely understood if we are to take advantage of the many opportunities it may present. Librarians should not simply be made to feel suffocated by the application of control beyond levels that they are familiar with. Any new funding or resource-sharing strategy should be considered for its potential benefit.

Collection development policies themselves have been the very instruments by which libraries have attempted to manage their local acquisition programs and collections, but this type of management has been self-imposed and is not the kind of control that I have in mind.

While I don't want to overdo an analogy with health care, it is the case that both information and health care share a number of similarities. Both are essential to the public good. Both health care and information services face substantial increases in costs that simply cannot be sustained through usual budget growth. Technology has been a major benefit in shaping and improving both services but it has also helped boost costs. Both health care and information services have experienced major increases in service demands, and attempts to manage the increased demands and costs have some striking similarities.

We are moving towards managed information just as surely as we have moved towards managed health care. Library funding entities have recognized that there is no way to keep up with the levels of service demands and the rise in costs without the application of management principles to control costs by urging libraries into arrangements that take more advantage of leveraged resources. These include consortial information purchases and more centralized coordination of what has been a very decentralized system of information acquisitions. Rather than providing additional funding to individual institutions for the acquisition of multiple copies of an information object to be located at duplicative sites, funding bodies are pooling limited dollars to promote the acquisition of collections and information services to be shared from central servers among the various participants in resource-sharing programs

In order to effectuate this policy, Information Management Organizations (IMOs) are being established among libraries just like their HMO counterparts have been established in health services.

The press of libraries into resource-sharing programs has been both subtle and overt. Where cooperation was once a choice that was left pretty much up to individual libraries, the new patterns that are emerging find multi-institutional funding bodies pushing libraries into arrangements for sharing local collections and access programs to distribute the cost of information acquisition, management, and delivery activities, while also improving the range and depth of information acquired.

While local institutions and libraries may still choose whether to participate or not in some of these extended resource-sharing programs, they will get special funding or benefits from other incentives that are being made available *only* if they buy into centrally managed information programs.

There are several examples of the application of this developing strategy. On a national level, the recent establishment of the AAU/ARL foreign acquisitions programs is an example that can be cited as a "soft" model of managed information.

In this model—encouraged by university presidents, the ARL, and foundation funding—libraries will assume responsibility for acquiring parts of the larger information universe while delegating the procurement of other pieces of that universe of knowledge to others. This represents a much larger commitment on a national basis than any we have had since the days of the Farmington Plan, the National Program for Acquisitions and Cataloging (NPAC), the Public Law 480 Program and the Latin American Cooperative Acquisitions Program (LACAP). Some programs were aimed at increasing duplication on an institution by institution basis, rather than simply ensuring that a copy would be acquired, cataloged and preserved for the many to share. These latter-day commitments to resource sharing are being encouraged at the institutional level, at a national organizational level, and at a funding level rather than being generated most specifically at the library level.

Similarly, other library organizations—on a regional, system or state level–are being pushed towards managed information programs. In my state of Texas, the TexShare library information-sharing program has been developed under the auspices of the Texas Council of State University Librarians. It has been funded at modest but helpful levels by the State Legislature, and those funds have been deeded to and are being managed by the Texas Higher Education Coordinating Board. In order to receive the most direct benefit of this funding, libraries are being asked to sign an agreement that they will participate in several specified statewide programs before they become eligible to receive funding or services being made available through the TexShare program.

These funds are indeed being leveraged to the advantage of the participants in the program. The costs of information delivery services are being reduced while the amount of information available to the participants is being increased, but libraries are having to give up a certain degree of independence in order to benefit from the managed information program.

A similar arrangement has been established among members of the University of Texas System libraries, whereby the fifteen academic and medical libraries in the UT System are utilizing funds made available from central System funds to participate in mutually agreed to, managed information service programs. It is increasingly more difficult for an institution to choose not to move its local library funding towards supporting commonly agreed to, shared programs if it wishes to gain any advantage from the seed funding from the central UT System source. These are not simply cooperative programs, they are efforts aimed at tightly managed coordinated activities.

Managed information programs that incorporate selection, budgeting, and fund allocation of network resources do not fit well with our existing models based on the $50 book or the $100 journal. The resources are more costly, decisions are more complex. Are the days of the lone bibliographer or scholar making decisions on their own for the mega-collections as numbered as the lone library making decisions on its own? Networking strains our organizational models and precepts, and obsolescent models and policies must give way to ones which best fit the fresh paradigm.

While a comprehensive survey is needed to fully assess the

degree to which managed information-sharing programs are being established on a national basis, a recent article in *The Chronicle of Higher Education* notes that "Statewide efforts already exist in Alabama, Georgia, Illinois, Louisiana, Ohio, Virginia, and Texas, while interstate groups have been formed among Big Ten research universities and among small liberal-arts colleges."[6]

I suspect that my description of managed information services will find a great deal of resonance among state-supported institutions participating in these programs, while private institutions may not feel as much top-down pressure for such consortial participation as do public ones.

Given that IMOs are already influencing the directions in which we acquire materials for our local collections as well as to share with one another, I can envision the application of still other management policies being added as riders to our funding authorizations. For example, many of us in the course of the establishment of resource-sharing programs have said: "You collect this, and I will collect that, and we will share those collections."

Might it not be a next logical step for a coordinating body to say to several of us in a state or university system: "All of you institutions offering graduate programs in biotechnology acquire one copy of a monograph and share it; all of you offering similar academic degree programs share in the cost of a subscription or an access license to digital information, and establish a physical or electronic carrier to distribute that information among yourselves."

In other words, do not just segregate collection responsibilities by institutional specialization, but aggregate institutionally by discipline offered and establish collection policies to reflect this practice. Never mind that the divisions of knowledge are inherently artificial, and contrary to the growth of interdisciplinary study and compound information. It should also be obvious that the establishment of standards and commonly agreed to collection and educational protocols in such an environment will be extremely difficult, but must be accomplished.

"And, oh, by the way," I hear that coordinating body saying, "you get only one professor to share among you in teaching this discipline and in directing research."

Distance learning is the hottest game in town and gown. It is in all of our library's best interests to ensure that policy makers understand that where distance learning goes it will require distance information as her hand-maiden.

SUMMARY

In summary, contemporary collection development policies must continue to be updated to reflect the actual practices and changes in the traditional building of local collections. They must also reflect the decisions that have been made to share collections through cooperative resource-sharing agreements, or to reveal the growing trans-consortial pressure of coordinating or funding agencies towards managed information and instructional programs.

Collection policies must recognize the evolving relationships between physical and digital information sources, and the creation of truly new multimedia or compound information objects that include text, graphics, sound, video and multi-dimensional animation—hyperlinked on a global basis.

The twenty-first century's system of information services and scholarship will be built on a new infrastructure that will be defined in our collection development policies. Elements included will be local acquisitions policy, collaborative agreements, managed information programs, networked collections and digital information, appropriate attention to copyright and intellectual property rights, cost-recovery-based services, and—if this structure is to stand—an economic framework unlike anything that presently exists.

Both library collections and distance information will be moving together towards digital center stage as this process unfolds in the years ahead.

NOTES

1. Anna H. Perrault, "Study Confirms Increased Homogeneity in Academic Library Acquisitions," *ARL: A Bimonthly Newsletter of Research Library Issues and Actions* 189 (May 1995): 5.

2. Anthony M. Cummings and others, *University Libraries and Scholarly Communication: A Study Prepared for the Andrew W. Mellon Foundation* (Washington: The Association of Research Libraries for The Andrew W. Mellon Foundation, 1992), 3.

3. Wm. A. Wulf, "Warning: Information Technology Will Transform the University," *Issues in Science and Technology* 11 (Summer 1995): 46-52.

4. Elizabeth Futas, ed., *Collection Development Policies and Procedures*. 3d ed. (Phoenix: Oryx Press, 1995).

5. Samuel Demas, Peter McDonald and Gregory Lawrence, "The Internet and Collection Development: Mainstreaming Selection of Internet Resources," *Library Resources & Technical Services* 39 (July 1995): 275-290.

6. Thomas J. DeLoughry, "Purchasing Power: Cost-sharing Efforts Help College Libraries Finance Electronic Acquisitions," *The Chronicle of Higher Education* 92 (Feb. 9, 1996): A21-A22.

Library Collections at Century's End: Lessons from American Express

Genevieve S. Owens

When I received the program for this conference and saw that my talk would immediately follow our keynote speaker's presentation, I was greatly relieved. This arrangement lets me complete the somewhat anxious task of presenting my thoughts at an early point in our proceedings. As I did some reading to prepare for today, however, I discovered that Sul and Don weren't just being kind when they scheduled my talk right after Harold's. I'm sure they were also aware of his piece on "The Tomorrow Librarian" in the January 1995 *Wilson Library Bulletin* and how well it leads into the thoughts I want to share with you today. In case you haven't read that article recently, it's a discussion of what Harold terms the "doomsday scenario for librarianship."[1] That scenario, promulgated in various professional and general publications, involves a future without us, a time when technologies either "replace and improve upon traditional libraries"[2] or wreak havoc on libraries and society at large. I confess to being irritated by these predictions, by disparaging questions about libraries' survival and future relevance. Then again, I tend to be irritated by disparaging questions about relevance in general. I was thoroughly annoyed, for example,

---

Genevieve S. Owens is Program Manager for Information Resources at Bucknell University in Lewisburg, PA.

[Haworth co-indexing entry note]: "Library Collections at Century's End: Lessons from American Express." Owens, Genevieve S. Co-published simultaneously in *Journal of Library Administration* (The Haworth Press, Inc.) Vol. 24, No. 1/2, 1996, pp. 19-33; and: *Emerging Patterns of Collection Development in Expanding Resource Sharing, Electronic Information and Network Environment* (ed: Sul H. Lee) The Haworth Press, Inc., 1996, pp. 19-33. Single or multiple copies of this article are available for a fee from The Haworth Document Delivery Service [1-800-342-9678, 9:00 a.m. - 5:00 p.m. (EST). E-mail address: getinfo@haworth.com].

by the April 1995 press conference in which a reporter had the impertinence to question Bill Clinton about the presidency's relevance. (Of course, in an age when the leader of the free world can be questioned about his underwear on MTV, such questions suddenly appear tame and polite.) As I think through my responses, however, I find that weak answers exasperate me more than rude questions. President Clinton stumbled by dignifying the underwear question with a response and by offering a vague reply to the query about his relevance. Harold Billings, I'm happy to report, doesn't miss a beat in the face of questioning, library doomsayers. He answers them with vigor. "I don't believe a word of it,"[3] he says of all those gloomy forecasts. He then goes on to tell us why we shouldn't, either.

In Harold's view and those of many other observers, we and our libraries will survive not in spite of but because of technology. Even in a fully digital environment, scholars will require assistance which machines simply can't offer. They will need librarians' interpretive, or what Ross Atkinson terms mediation, skills. The tricky part, Atkinson notes, is not the far-distant future but this slippery transition time, this era in which new and traditional library resources co-exist and people ask those irritating questions about our relevance. What tactics should we employ in this transition? Atkinson advises against bristling, self-defensive strategies. "The primary goal of the library," he says, "must not be survival but information services. Study the changing information needs of the academic community, design services that will meet those needs more effectively than services offered by other agencies inside or outside of academe, and survival will take care of itself."[4] In other, more cinematic words, "If you build it, they will come."

To build services our users prefer, librarians must operate with an outward orientation, an emphasis on our patrons rather than internal library processes. I believe many of us are developing this orientation already. In the realm of collections, for example, I observe an increasing concern with materials' practical utility. This concern is not entirely native to collection builders, of course. Much of it has been foisted upon us by financial circumstances. Our libraries simply cannot afford to amass huge collections anymore. Even when we're dealing with desirable, high-quality materials that we used to collect for their own sake, we must now consider the specific needs those items will meet and their overall cost-effectiveness. Given the fact that this orientation is a relatively new and largely imposed one, it is not likely to flourish without some careful attention. That attention should take many forms, including the introspection and self-examination which fill the library literature. There are moments, however, when introspection becomes a form of withdrawal, retreat instead of renewal. Lately, as I have worked on an annotated collection management bibliography, I've needed a perspective from outside our camp, one which teaches me about that outward orientation in an unexpected, very memorable way. I've found that lesson in a piece of plastic, the American Express card.

Let me begin this admittedly unorthodox discussion with some background on the famous green (or gold or platinum) card. In plain terms, it's in trouble. In 1990, American Express claimed 24.8 percent of the U.S. card market share. By mid-year 1995, its market share had plunged to 16.1 percent.[5] Why this precipitous drop? It's being edged out by the competition. As all of us surely know, the American Express card is a charge card. Customers pay an annual fee for it, and they must pay their bills in full each month. The card's principle advantages are its lack of a preset spending limit and its prestige. Customers equate the American Express card with both reliability and luxury; many people even equate the card with the company itself. American Express, a diversified travel and financial services company, has made the most of these associations. Its name is now "one of the ten most-recognized brands in the world."[6]

VISA and MasterCard, the products which gobbled up most of Amex's market share losses, are credit cards. They charge no annual fees (banks will usually waive such fees on request), and they allow customers to carry a balance from month to month. Credit cards have several disadvantages, beginning with their spending ceilings. Cardholders with adequate limits, however, can get as much functionality from those products as American Express cards without paying an annual fee. Customers give up some prestige by choosing VISA or MasterCard, to be sure, but that factor's influence is waning in the face of credit cards' aggressive advertising campaigns and consumers' increasing intolerance for annual fees.

Consumer intolerance is not a factor, on the other hand, when it comes to credit cards' other major drawback, their hefty interest rates. Those rates make the credit card market extremely lucrative right now. Issuers borrow money at around 7 percent and generally loan it to cardholders at about 17 percent. That's a spread made in financiers' dreams. Card issuers get away with it because consumers tend to deny the size of their balances and the amount of interest they're actually paying. Given consumers' waning interest in a card's prestige, their disdain for annual fees, and credit cards' bizarre psychological effects, it's no wonder that American Express is having such difficulties.[7]

But what about libraries' market share? Are our customers leaving us in droves, lured away by the charms of other information providers? Certainly not to the degree that they're leaving American Express for MasterCard and VISA. In public libraries, in fact, a recent *U.S. News and World Report* poll shows that the opposite is true. That study found "67 percent of American adults went to a [public] library at least once in the past year–up markedly from the 51 percent who visited in 1978."[8] Among those polled, moreover, "only 8 percent think computers will render libraries obsolete; 91 percent say libraries will still be needed."[9]

In academic libraries, the market share question is more tricky. The ARL statistics, for example, clearly show increases in our student and faculty populations, but it's hard to tell how many of them our libraries are actually serving. We're certainly borrowing a breathtaking amount of material for users via interlibrary loan, but that pattern may simply reflect our shrinking local collections.[10] The ARL has just begun to track and publish other measures of library use like reference and circulation transactions; it will be interesting to see what those numbers look like over the next few years. My own experience tells me that the figures are likely to hold steady or even drop from year to year. Again, it's hard to know what to make of such trends. They may reflect decreasing library use or they may simply reflect changing use patterns. Circulation figures, for example, might easily drop as a result of increased reliance on electronic full-text sources. Even if some upward trends do emerge,

I'm concerned about situations where researchers go out and purchase materials which the library already owns or has specifically chosen not buy. In some instances, of course, such purchases are entirely appropriate. In other cases, however, these situations represent end-runs around libraries and diminish our position as central information providers. While some of my concern stems from anecdotal evidence, it is also supported by Christa Reinke's research at the University of Michigan. She notes significant overlaps between library holdings and materials purchased by individual departments at that institution, particularly in the areas of science, technology, and medicine. Her study demonstrates the lengths to which our users may go for more relevant materials or more convenient access to them than libraries can provide.[11]

Intriguing as market share studies may be, we really don't need them to understand the life cycles of corporations or libraries. When businesses are left on automatic pilot, when libraries are allowed to do what they've always done, the results are the same. Both operations will decline and ultimately fall. American Express continued on in the same old way until it was almost too late. It took the loss of 2.2 million card holders to alert the company to the necessity of doing things differently. Businesses with less recognized brands, and I include libraries in that group, can't afford to sustain such losses. Regardless of our current market shares, we simply must find ways to change with technology and with our users.

Cultivating change is no easy matter, but it's proved especially difficult at American Express. The company is legendary for its arrogance and inability to move quickly. In the mid-1980s, for example, American Airlines approached Amex about the possibility of creating a co-branded card, one which awarded consumers with a frequent-flier mile for every dollar they charged. American Express turned the airline down cold; the company wasn't interested in sharing the face of its card with anyone. A decade later, the phenomenal success of the General Motors card—the one which provides a rebate on the purchase of a GM car—and others like it demonstrate the folly of this attitude.[12]

At the risk of offending everyone in this room, I suggest that there are moments when librarians are guilty of the arrogance which threatens to topple a corporate giant like American Express. As one who lives in a glass house, I'll throw the first stone at myself for bristling at questions about libraries' relevance. In defense of my kind, let me also suggest that arrogance or one of its related attributes is something of an occupational hazard for collection managers. Each and every day, we make decisions about what will and will not be kept in our libraries, about what stays and what goes. We often make those decisions after consulting patrons, other librarians, and selection tools. We may even allow material–in some cases, lots of it–to enter or leave our collections without our personal review. At the end of the day, however, at some fundamental level, we are responsible for saving materials from or relegating them to oblivion. Yes, it sounds grandiose, and I don't think of my work in those terms very often. Still, it takes expertise and a large dose of chutzpah to make the choices we make day in and day out. If you don't believe me, spend an hour with a new selector and some approval books. Watch how the decisions you'd make with ease, even in subject areas you don't know, are really hard for that librarian. I'm sure the decision-making strategies I share with new selectors make me seem opinionated and occasionally arbitrary. For collection managers, however, these qualities are often survival skills, not character flaws. Harvey Golub, American Express's CEO, notes a similar situation in his organization. "It's a fine line," he says, "and I'm sure that to some people what may be viewed as confidence comes across as arrogance. To others it comes across as humility. If we had everybody saying we're not arrogant, my guess is we would be servile."[13]

Acknowledging that confidence *is* arrogance if we fail to address change, I'm going to explore three areas in which American Express and its recovery strategies speak to those of us in the library business. At the outset, I should warn you that each of these strategies is a marketing move. The word "marketing" has unpleasant connotations for many of us. I know I associate it with efforts to get people to buy things they neither want nor need. In some cases, marketing is amusing and innocuous. On the Bucknell University campus, for example, the fashion industry has persuaded many young women that unattractive, 1970s clothing styles are wearable and contemporary. In other instances, marketing is an annoyance. Telemarketing wins the gold medal in this category. And in still other cases, marketing is immoral and deserves to be met with resistance movements like boycotts. In all of these examples, however, I'm confusing marketing with one of its more specific functions, namely sales and promotion. Marketing, as business books say, is an all-encompassing term which refers to the use of a company's resources to supply wanted goods and services at a profit. It requires the mastery of a host of different operations, from product design to pricing to distribution to promotion. Marketing is characterized by its emphasis on customers' point of view, on customers' needs and wants.[14] It's very much in keeping with the outward orientation our libraries should have.

Librarians have actually been interested in marketing since the late nineteenth century. Recent years, moreover, have witnessed the publication of at least two major works on the topic. The Winter 1995 issue of *Library Trends* was titled, "Marketing of Library and Information Services." In 1993, Sharon L. Baker treated collections from a marketing standpoint in *The Responsive Public Library Collection: How to Develop and Market It*.[15] Public librarians and library school faculty do tend to be the ones most interested in marketing, and that interest makes a good deal of sense. Public libraries' audiences are far less captive than academic libraries' patrons. One more merger, and the entertainment industry could gobble up a chunk of public library users in a single bite. Indeed, the captive audience factor is one of the reasons I tend to dismiss the doomsday scenario for academic libraries. Our stock and trade—scholarly information—is not going to be acquired by the Disney Corporation any time soon. As my observations about end-run purchases indicate, however, even captive audiences find ways to escape when our marketing focus wavers and we no longer meet our patrons' needs.

Now that I've disabused us of the notion that marketing is entirely loathsome, on to some marketing lessons from American Express. The first lesson is co-branding, offering a new product under two partnered yet entirely independent brand names. Yes, a decade after it sent American Airlines packing and began its downward spiral, the company has teamed up with Delta Air Lines to offer the Delta SkyMiles Optima credit card. Delta was the last major carrier without its own card. Amex's deal with them is something of a coup because other card companies were vying for the partnership, too.[16] Since Kit and Becky's talks both have some variation of the word "partner" in their titles, I'll try not steal any of their thunder by elaborating on this lesson too much. On the whole, I believe our libraries have not been as guilty of arrogance in this department as American Express. Looking at resource sharing, for example, I believe our partnering intentions are noble, even if the product leaves something to be desired. We all have formed partnerships with vendors as well, sharing the faces of our library cards with book jobbers and serials vendors and database providers in spirit if not in fact.

Choosing the right partners for our cards is always a tricky matter, but it's especially difficult to make those choices from an outwardly focused, library marketing perspective. It's one thing, in other words, to choose a partner on the basis of librarians' preferences and standards. It can be a very different thing to choose a partner who will best meet library users' needs and desires. As a collections librarian, for example, I am most interested in a journal table of contents service's coverage, in the titles it carries, and the articles it can deliver from those titles. From a marketing perspective, however, the service with the most suitable coverage and delivery may not be the best choice for my library. Perhaps the means of accessing it is so clumsy or the interface is so bad that faculty give up on it in disgust. Perhaps it's not a question of content or access but the service's name-recognition. In my previous position, the faculty were so devoted to *Current Contents* that they wouldn't accept an alternative table of contents service from God. Such considerations may seem trivial until we remember that we're not always providing these services as supplements to our holdings. As Chuck will elaborate shortly, we're often providing them as substitutes–very cost effective ones–for those holdings. A move like that is riddled with public relations landmines. We need to step through those landmines with partners who won't lead us into fatal marketing stumbles.

Moving from deadly explosions to more positive ones, American Express lesson number two is a burst of brand extension. This strategy involves the launch of new products under a single company's existing, successful brand name. American Express is pursuing many brand extension projects right now, but I'm going to focus on the Optima card and the Optima True Grace card.

Like the Delta SkyMiles card, both Optima products are credit cards. All three credit cards represent Amex's attempts to cash in on those wonderful interest rate spreads I mentioned earlier. Some analysts think that American Express has entered the credit card business too late, that the party there is almost over as super low-cost VISA and MasterCards come on the market. Failure lurks around other corners as well. Remember the prestige of the American Express charge card? Well, that prestige and its remaining customer base could erode even further if Amex becomes too closely associated with the commonplace world of credit cards. Everyday credit cardholders, on the other hand, may not take too kindly to the snob appeal of these new Amex products, even if they're printed in blue to distinguish them from the charge plates. So far, the Optima True Grace card has actually done quite well. Market watchers attribute its performance to an advertising campaign featuring Martha Stewart.[17] She seems to strike the right balance between uppity and folksy, retiling the pool, but doing it herself with cut-up credit cards now that she's found True Grace.

What new products are libraries offering and what risks do they pose for us? I'm sure there are many interesting examples. At the moment, the one which strikes me is the multimedia collection at Bucknell University's Bertrand Library. It's a small collection, about 150 titles right now, but it's relatively unique for an academic library. Just in case it's unique enough to be obscure, let me explain that it's a collection of interactive CD-ROMs which incorporate text and graphics and sometimes sound and video clips. If you've ever used Microsoft's *Encarta Encyclopedia*, you've used a multimedia product. Patrons can check out the discs for three days. The library has a lab, shared with our Modern Foreign Languages Department, where patrons can use the products. Since most new desktop computer packages include CD-ROM drives, we're also finding that more and more of our patrons can use the titles at home or in their offices.

The Bertrand Library's multimedia collection is a progressive, even visionary one. It's a fine illustration of the library's commitment to collecting on the basis of materials' content rather than their format. In fairness to libraries without multimedia, Bucknell's setting may be more conducive to this collection than other institutions' environments. For one thing, we have a relatively adequate budget for books and other one-time purchases. Thanks to the protective efforts of library administrators, that budget has not been siphoned off to satisfy the insatiable demands of our serials costs. Second, by working creatively with Modern Foreign Languages when they expressed interest in the library's space, we obtained a multimedia lab that we probably couldn't afford otherwise. Finally, the University's Instructional Media Services unit reports to the library director, and we have a media resources librarian who coordinates our collecting in this area. This organizational structure helps to keep media in the forefront of our awareness. Despite these situational advantages, the multimedia collection would not exist without the willingness to think ahead of the curve or at least along with it. The library saw these products, realized that they meet some of our patrons' needs, and took entrepreneurial action to fulfill those needs. Unlike American Express and its credit cards, we are not showing up as the party winds down to a close. In fact, we're among the first library guests to arrive.

I have concerns, however, about the kind of party multimedia is hosting, and here is where the risks come into play. As John McChesney reported on NPR's "Morning Edition" a few weeks ago, the multimedia industry is still in its infancy. Most of its output consists of products designed and priced for the home consumer market. Given the explosion of the World Wide Web, another sort of interactive hypermedia, the future of multimedia on CD-ROM is not entirely clear.[18] If multimedia is in fact eclipsed by the Web, the Bertrand Library could find itself with twenty-first century equivalents of microcards, materials in search of a machine on which they can be read. This situation would certainly not be a first among libraries, nor would it represent a huge financial loss given the materials' relatively low cost. After many experiences with new formats, moreover, the library community is finally taking steps to develop archival and refreshing techniques for many different kinds of data.

While multimedia poses some preservation risks, I believe it raises even more serious questions. These questions concern the implications of interactive media in general, the meaning of clicking from link to link, amongst text and pictures and sound and film clips and whatever else developers can load onto multimedia products or even World Wide Web sites. I have very mixed reactions to these creations. In some applications, largely artists' projects, the technology's positive features are incontrovertible. It provides marvelous avenues for a full range of creative sensibilities. In other cases, I can see why proponents are excited about the technology's educational potential, how, in Taylor Hubbard's words, it allows us to "alter, embellish, comment on, and criticize the subject of study."[19] At the risk of sounding utterly retrograde, however, I'm concerned that interactive media may just be another form of the daily information overload. We tend to manage that overload by surfing with our various remote controls, sampling and learning a great deal of nothing. It's fine to genuinely respond to texts rather than receiving wisdom from on high, but that activity requires an attention span, intellectual rigor and discipline. I'm not convinced that interactive media creations promote these fundamental skills, and I genuinely wonder about the cultural messages which point and click technologies convey.

Turning this discussion of basics back to American Express, the company's third and final lesson involves market segmentation strategies aimed at its basic, original card. Market segmentation, tailoring products to meet the needs of an especially promising group of customers, makes sense for the American Express card. Its customers generally charge two and a half times more purchases each year than credit card holders,[20] and these purchases generate a significant amount of merchant fee income for the company. In this instance, American Express plans to capitalize on one of its unique advantages, its transaction system. Unlike VISA or MasterCard, where transactions run through many different banks and data transmission systems, the American Express card operates in a closed-loop network. American Express "handles every step of its cardholder and merchant transactions, from the actual charge to the final billing."[21] This structure means that American Express has a huge database of information on its cardholders' purchasing habits. VISA and MasterCard, on the other hand, have this information widely scattered throughout their systems with little hope of effective retrieval.

Recognizing the potential of its database, American Express has embarked on an ambitious campaign to capitalize on its position. In the past year, the company has spent an undisclosed sum on the purchase of new software and computing equipment. This technology will allow it to produce customized marketing programs in a matter of days, not the weeks or months those programs required in the recent past. Using its new systems, Amex will be offering cardholders special promotions on products and services they tend to purchase anyway.[22] Promotions might include discounts at particular types of restaurants or individual hotel chains, or special offers on travel to certain parts of the world. The important point is that these offers will be targeted to a group of likely consumers; they will not be offered indiscriminately to cardholders at large. If this approach works, as it has in European test markets, it will be advantageous for cardholders, merchants, and Amex alike. Customers will receive added value from their cards, merchants will benefit from strategically targeted promotions, and American Express will both solidify and eventually increase its market share as word of the card's benefits spreads.

It's not difficult to make the leap from the American Express database to the ones in our libraries. Our libraries, after all, are closed-loop systems, too. Even in union catalog or statewide network situations, our bibliographic and transaction information exists or can be extracted in complete, confined ways; it's not hopelessly scattered. It's also easy to see parallels between the hurdles American Express faces in making use of its database and the ones our libraries encounter. Let's assume, for example, that we want to make full use of the wealth of information in our circulation files. The first hurdle will be coaxing that information out of our computers in useful formats. As Stephen Atkins notes in a recent article on "Mining Automated Systems for Collection Management," vendors have been slow to develop the reporting features of their products. While systems are offering an increasing number of preformatted reports, libraries often need more flexibility than canned programs can provide. Even when more flexible reporting software is available, that software tends to require expert attention from a programmer, and programmers' attention must often be fixed on other aspects of systems operation.[23] Is more flexible reporting worth an American Express-style investment in supercomputers and wildly expensive software? Probably not, and even if it were, I doubt our libraries could afford or justify such expenditures in the face of competing financial pressures. The point, however, is that library systems' reporting functions matter a great deal in a marketing approach to collection management. Since that approach is a key to libraries' future, those functions must assume a more important place in system vendors' development plans and in the criteria libraries use to make decisions about those systems.

Considering the very targeted promotions American Express plans to produce with its new computer systems, analysts note that the rewards program may strike cardholders as an invasion of privacy. It is based after all, on "an electronic trail of their purchases."[24] I'm not sure what to make of this concern. On the one hand, it seems rather frivolous. Certainly most of us, especially upscale cardholders, realize that this sort of personal information is available *everywhere* in this wired world of ours. Why not have some of that information put to good use in the form of discounts on things we're going to buy anyway? On the other hand, it doesn't take much for me to become really worried about all that wired, personal information. My recent splurge at Nordstrom is one thing; my medical history is quite another. At the very least, American Express would be well-advised to allow cardholders to remove themselves from the rewards program if they choose.

While privacy may not be a big issue at American Express, it certainly is in libraries. In a recent *Library Journal* article, Leigh Estabrook notes that "to guard the privacy and confidentiality of data relating to library users is to act on one of our most cherished values as librarians."[25] She points out, however, that "librarians' obsession with confidentiality of patron records is actually relatively new. It came about only after the implementation of library automation."[26] Dean Estabrook devotes the rest of her article to considering all the wonderful, market-oriented things libraries could do with circulation and other data about patrons' preferences and interests. She talks about automated patron surveys, user profiles, reference service, and promotion campaigns. While pointing out the need for patrons' "informed consent"[27] and mechanisms which conceal their identity, she argues that libraries should make use of the data in our own "closed-loops." Like the information at American Express, that data can give libraries an advantage over our competitors.

I've just discussed three strategies—co-branding, brand extension, and market segmentation—which American Express is using to preserve its role in a rapidly changing environment, and I've considered ways to apply them to library collections. Are these tactics working for American Express? The jury's still out, but the company's earnings were up 14.6 percent in the fourth quarter as card use rose.[28] In an even more telling move, famed investor Warren Buffet has purchased nearly two billion dollars of American Express shares. Buffet, who chooses stocks he believes are temporarily undervalued, is banking on Amex's ability to ride out the storm of industry change on the back of smart marketing and its strong brand.[29]

Do libraries have what it takes to weather storms of change? Like Harold Billings, I believe we do. Our brand admittedly doesn't rival the one at American Express. Faculty and students have been know to leave home without us, and that "heart of the University" advertising slogan has been shopworn for some time now. But we don't need worldwide recognition to survive. We merely need vision that is clear enough to focus on our users and sharp enough to spot ways of doing that, even when those ways appear in highly unlikely places.

NOTES

1. Harold Billings, "The Tomorrow Librarian," *Wilson Library Bulletin* 69 (January 1995): 34.
2. Ibid., 35.
3. Ibid., 34.
4. Ross Atkinson, "Access, Ownership, and the Future of Collection Development," in *Collection Management and Development: Issues in an Electronic Era*, ed. Peggy Johnson and Bonnie MacEwan (Chicago: American Library Association, 1994), 92-93.
5. Linda Grant, "Why Warren Buffett's Betting Big on American Express," *Fortune*, October 30, 1995, 72.
6. Ibid., 70.

7. Ibid., 78.

8. "The Resilient Library," *U.S. News & World Report*, December 11, 1995, 29.

9. Ibid.

10. *1993-94 ARL Statistics* (Washington, D.C.: Association of Research Libraries, 1995).

11. Christa Easton Reinke, "Beyond the Fringe: Administratively Decentralized Collections at the University of Michigan," *Library Acquisitions: Practice & Theory* 18 (Summer 1994): 157-64.

12. Stephen D. Solomon, "American Express Applies for a New Line of Credit," *New York Times Magazine*, July 30, 1995, 36.

13. Linda Grant, "American Express," 72.

14. Lee Adler, "Marketing," in *The Encyclopedia of Management*, 3d ed., ed. Carl Heyel (New York: Van Nostrand Reinhold, 1982), 653-656.

15. Englewood, Colo.: Libraries Unlimited, 1993.

16. Linda Grant, "American Express," 84.

17. Ibid.

18. National Public Radio, "Morning Edition," February 23, 1996, Transcript # 1810-12.

19. Taylor E. Hubbard, "Bibliographic Instruction and Postmodern Pedagogy," *Library Trends* 44 (Fall 1995): 449.

20. Linda Grant, "American Express," 82.

21. Stephen D. Solomon, "American Express," 44.

22. Kate Fitzgerald, "Marketers Capture Prospects Using AmEx 'Closed Loop'," *Advertising Age*, October 9, 1995, 18.

23. Stephen Atkins, "Mining Automated Systems for Collection Management," *Library Administration & Management* 10 (Winter 1996): 16-19.

24. Stephen D. Solomon, "American Express," 47.

25. Leigh S. Estabrook, "Sacred Trust or Competitive Opportunity: Using Patron Records," *Library Journal*, February 1, 1996, 48.

26. Ibid.

27. Ibid., 49.

28. *New York Times*, 23 January 1996, sec. D, p. 6.

29. Linda Grant, "American Express," 78.

Designing Serial Collections for the 21st Century

Charles Hamaker

LSU Libraries, in 1994, was NOT planning on a cancellation in 1995. We were not interested in deciding what MORE to cancel of our rapidly dwindling serials collection, what we were concerned about was how best to use the resources we had to meet the educational and research needs of our faculty and students. That is STILL our primary concern, even in a year when we have had to meet a 15% increase in the cost of our serials. I know, in the midst of pressures to "cancel" it is hard to keep this in perspective, because all the resources are going to meet an immediate deadline.

What we DID plan was for almost every area of the library to become involved in meeting the needs for cost-effective access to research information. From public services and selectors, to interlibrary borrowing to technical services to systems. From the Dean of Libraries and the Vice Chancellor of Academic Affairs, to programmers developing a customized clipper database, almost every level of staff was involved in developing solutions to a critical problem, one too often addressed by collection development librarians and serials librarians and faculty by themselves.

Why was it a library-wide plan? Because it was and is a library-

---

Charles Hamaker is Assistant Dean for Collection Development at Louisiana State University in Baton Rouge, LA.

[Haworth co-indexing entry note]: "Designing Serial Collections for the 21st Century." Hamaker, Charles. Co-published simultaneously in *Journal of Library Administration* (The Haworth Press, Inc.) Vol. 24, No. 1/2, 1996, pp. 35-46; and: *Emerging Patterns of Collection Development in Expanding Resource Sharing, Electronic Information and Network Environment* (ed: Sul H. Lee) The Haworth Press, Inc., 1996, pp. 35-46. Single or multiple copies of this article are available for a fee from The Haworth Document Delivery Service [1-800-342-9678, 9:00 a.m. - 5:00 p.m. (EST). E-mail address: getinfo@haworth.com].

and, indeed, university-wide problem. It is a problem for the whole academy. Kendon Stubbs in the new 1994-1995 *ARL Statistics* states it succinctly: "libraries, publishers, and authors seem unable to put an end to this cycle (of serial crisis)." Since 1986 the Median ARL expenditure for serials has risen from 1.5 million dollars to 3.1 million dollars, more than doubling, while the unit price of a serial in ARL libraries has risen from $88.81 to $221.29. If this were to continue, we would assume the Median expenditure for serials in ARL libraries will rise to over 6 million dollars within the next decade! I predict this will not happen. This year a trend seen in previous years has accelerated. ARL libraries report 8% fewer subscriptions than they did in 1986. For years the level of book purchasing has dropped, today down 23% from 10 years ago. And now subscription levels have begun to drop.

Frankly, given what we have just learned from our intensive faculty survey, this does not alarm me. Let me give you some reasons for that. First, I want to explain that in the last two papers I've given here, I've talked about how we surveyed our faculty. I don't intend to discuss that in the formal presentation, but will be happy to answer any questions about it in the question and answer period.

WHAT DID WE LEARN?

The 400 science, engineering and agricultural sciences faculty who participated in the survey (about a 50% return rate) identified 2,689 journals they felt we needed subscriptions to. We had subscriptions to 1,675 of those journals, and there were 954 titles (with a cost of $413,708) they wanted which we did not own. But we also found that we had subscriptions to over 300 titles in the sciences that, though they had been defended by various departments with varying degrees of fervor over the last decade of cancellations reviews, were not of specific interest to ANY of our faculty. That equated to $120,000 in titles that no single faculty member needed, though they had been spared in previous rounds. I can tell you that cancellation list was the easiest list I have ever sent out in all my years as a librarian.

The "complaints" were almost non-existent. One faculty member claimed he needed a $3,500 journal that somehow he hadn't bothered to mention in filling out his survey. And one department chair speaking for about 10 faculty claimed a slew of titles that obviously his department needed. Well, to be honest, I ignored both of those responses. Because the Chair couldn't really tell me WHICH faculty member needed which title, just that they all needed all of them. One of them we hadn't received for over 14 months (though paid for), and it was very expensive, so I have to admit, that if pushed, I would suggest that neither the chair nor whomever he was speaking for evidenced much real knowledge of that title. As for the $3,500 journal, I'm prepared to offer a document delivery account or a book fund equivalent to that (or some mixture) if really pushed. But in reality, we are going to watch what happens, now that faculty and graduate students can order articles directly to their own FAX machines from UnCover.

I've been criticized for this cavalier attitude by those who claim they are building archival collections. I have to admit, I AM NOT building an archival collection of Elsevier journals, or Pergamon journals, or AIP journals, or any other major publisher's titles. LSU is NOT the archival collection for standard physics titles, for mega dollar pharmacology titles, for a whole range of areas, where, I admit, 10 years ago we believed we had some kind of sacred responsibility. *Brain Research* is NOT LSU's responsibility. It is not the "archival" responsibility of each of the ARL libraries, nor even a significant portion of them. But they haven't figured that out yet. And Elsevier would just as soon we all thought we were protecting it for the next millennium.

I have it on excellent authority that Pergamon, for example, has a complete archival set of everything it has ever published. So don't worry about their titles. They will survive. There are titles that we SHOULD be worrying about, but the top of the line increasingly expensive science journals are NOT the ones we need to be concerned about. Honest. For North America, and perhaps the western hemisphere, the *Official Australian Cane Growers Guide* probably is LSU's responsibility.

Let me give you some numbers that are behind some of these heretical notions. Basic Sciences is probably our most active college in terms of grants, research support, and thinking about BIG science. In it are Physics/Astronomy, Chemistry, Zoology/Physiology, Biochemistry, Plant Biology, Computer Science, Geology and Geophysics, and about 181 faculty, 103 of whom responded to our survey. They identified a total of 383 journals that we do not own that they are interested in. What I found astounding was that for 95 of those journals (and yes, I checked, they are mainstream science journals), or 24%, they believed that an access system would be sufficient for their needs. Another fact I found interesting is that the average price of the journals they wanted access to was about $594, while the average price of the journals they wanted purchased was $358. The college represented 38% of the dollar total desired for new subscriptions, 25% of the faculty who participated, and their titles were 35% of the new titles recommended.

In Biochemistry, 8 of the 10 faculty participated in the survey, and identified a total of 64 journals we HAVE subscriptions to as of interest to them. However, 17 of those titles, again 26%, were ONLY of interest to them via document delivery. All of those journals cost $73,299, but those they wanted for document delivery cost $28,913, or 39% of the total dollar amount. This would have been even higher, but ONE of the 8 faculty felt that *FEBS Letters* ($3,084 worth) should be a subscription. The other 7 wanted it via document delivery. That is, for this particular faculty, half of the dollar amount of stuff we are already buying to support them, they didn't feel it was necessary to own!

Geology and Geophysics identified 106 journals of interest that we currently subscribe to. However, 45% of those titles are only of interest to a single faculty member.

In fact, for our whole list of titles, 44% of the titles identified as needed in-house, via subscription, were only of interest to a SINGLE faculty member. Now think about the implications of that: 44% of the titles WE OWN are only of interest to a single faculty member. Doesn't that suggest that those titles, dearly beloved as they might be, should be investigated in some detail as to the cost effectiveness to the INSTITUTION of retaining them? Here is another number to consider. The average faculty member in our survey identified 28 journals needed, 21 of them recommended for subscription. NINE of those 21 journals are ONLY of interest to the individual faculty member. I've been looking at these numbers since June of last year, and I am still working my way towards understanding what they mean. For the library, for the university, for the academy, and yes, whether they want to hear it or not, for publishers of some very expensive journals hard questions must be asked. Because, in fact, if these numbers hold up across types of journals and remember we were only surveying the "science" piece of our campus, they represent, in my opinion, an incredible waste of resources. For many of the most expensive titles, though not all, we are serving a very small segment of our primary clientele at a very high price.

I recently had a question from our electronic services librarian. We, as I am sure many of you, had a "free" subscription through OCLC for one of the physics titles we subscribe to in paper. Time for the "freebie" was over and the question was, did we want to pay the "extra" for the electronic version. It turned out that the title had been "hit" or accessed through our web-server by our patrons 150 times. It also turned out that OCLC couldn't tell us how many other uses there were on "our" password, i.e., through faculty or students going to the title by other means. But I thought, wow, what a bargain, for only $150 more we KNOW that it was accessed 150 times!

That's a dollar a hit. One of the biggest bargains I've ever heard of in the sciences. But of course, that wasn't the cost of those hits. It was actually the cost of the paper journal plus the lagniappe price. But even at that, I was impressed that ANY version of the journal or that the combined versions of the journal were accessed that much. However, you have to ask (and I may be wrong about the price of the journal) if that was ALL the access, ALL the need, what did it really cost. And my guess is that our use per-use access of the combined paper and electronic version was in the $20.00 per "hit" range, and that's ignoring our processing costs. I still think it was a bargain.

But this leads me to the "other" question raised by a lot of people over the data in the *Forbes* (Dec. 18, 1995) article. You can see, I would guess, given the 44% figure I've given you, why cancelling a single title may not mean much in terms of lost utility to the collection. In fact, this whole area, utility cost, is going to have to be looked at individually in just about every major library for titles where the cost of maintaining traditional access, i.e., in-house, is extremely high, and where cost increases are running 3 or 4 times inflation. By the way, Stubbs, in the preface to the new *ARL Statistics*, says the serial unit price, cost per title is now averaging a price increase level of 11.4% per year! As you all know, this cost increase is NOT across the board, but highly concentrated in the hands of very specific publishers. At this stage, after a decade of "serials crisis," I don't even need to mention who those publishers are.

But I do need to mention something of a solution besides trying to figure out how to get that last marginal title away from that last protective professor–if this were e-mail I'd put a smiley after that to let you know I'm only half serious :-). You all know by now that in 1993 we cancelled $446,000 worth of journals. AND offered to buy articles for ANY of those journals we had canceled for any faculty or graduate student who needed them. The results are pretty astounding. I have an overhead that shows what we learned from this experience (Figure 1). We ordered articles from 936 journals, at a total cost $26,216.54. We ordered 2,092 articles, copyright fee was $12,618.54 and delivery cost (via fax) was $13,598. However, as the graph shows, 594 of those journals we only ordered ONE article from. There were 20 journals in all that we ordered 10 or more articles from, and in fact, they are interesting for a number of reasons. Of those "top 20" we never had subscription to 17 of the titles. And one of the titles we have a current subscription to. Two of the titles we had actually cancelled in 1992, and the number one almost cost as much as the subscription title, the one we ordered 100 articles from, actually, for 1995 cost $1,300, or the same as our cost in copyright plus delivery fee. This one is really funny, because most of this ordering was for one graduate student. I, of course, was very interested in what our faculty survey showed on this title. Would it surprise you if I told you that the 6 faculty who listed it weren't even in the same college as our graduate student? Now, don't think for a minute that a single year's subscription would have met our needs. In fact, the articles ordered were from the last 4 years. So our investment to meet that need would be around $5,000. And that, my friends, is the ONLY title that came anywhere close to equaling the subscription price in document delivery costs. I have put down at the bottom of Figure 2, the total copyright we paid in

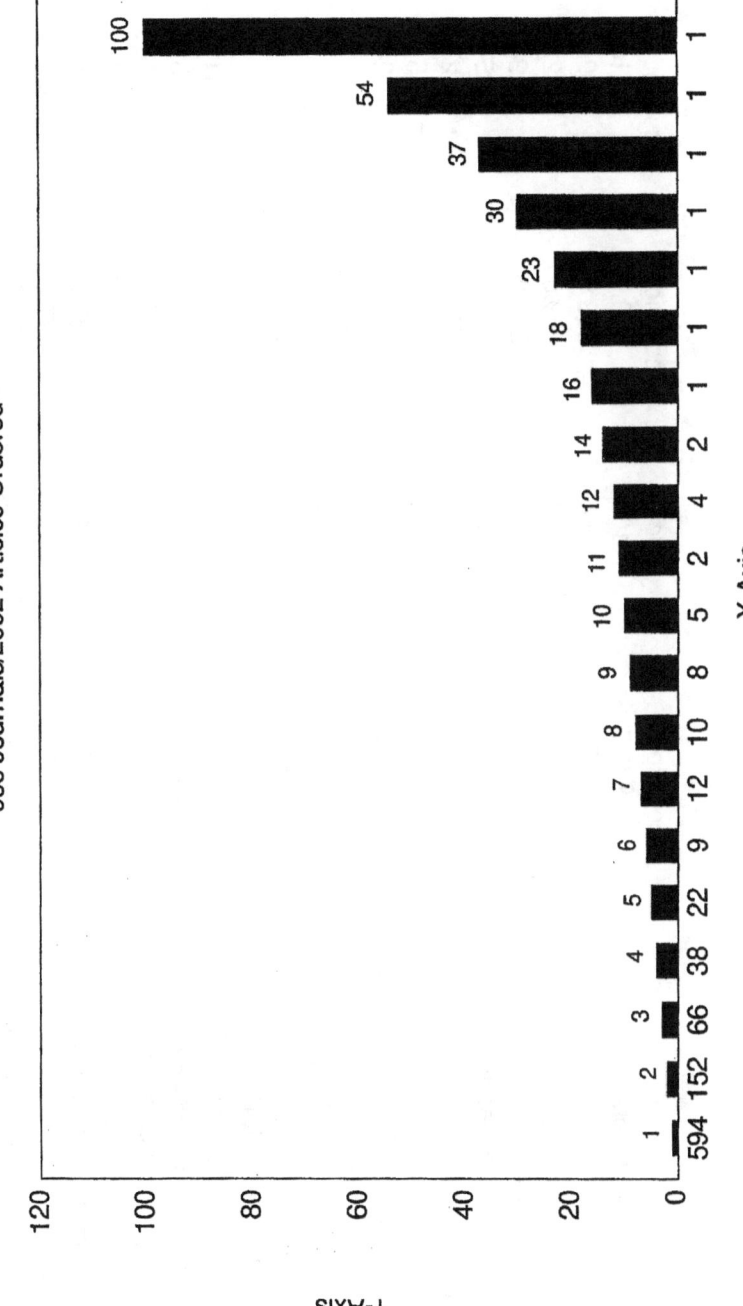

FIGURE 2

	copyright	orders	copyright	subscription
Sensors and actuators. Pt. A	$7.00	100	700.00	$1,184
Automatica	$7.00	54	378.00	$985
European journal of pharmacology	$7.00	37	259.00	$4,222
Neuroscience letters	$7.00	30	210.00	$2,943
Scripta metallurgica et materialia	$7.00	23	161.00	$570
Planta medica	$4.25	18	76.50	$278
Environmental toxicology and chem	$7.00	16	112.00	$515
American journal of industrial medi	$9.00	14	126.00	$1,289
Psychopharmacology	$6.00	14	84.00	$2,363
Applied catalysis. A, General	$7.00	12	84.00	$2,921
Journal of environmental quality	$0.90	12	10.80	
Personality and individual differen	$7.00	12	84.00	$710
Sensors and actuators. Pt. B	$7.00	12	84.00	$1,115
International journal of peptide an	$10.25	11	112.75	$520
Toxicology and industrial health	$3.25	11	35.75	$168
Mechanism and machine theory	$7.00	10	70.00	$900
Neuropsychiatry, neuropsychology,	$6.25	10	62.50	$174
Neuroscience	$7.00	10	70.00	$3,035
Science of the total environment	$7.00	10	70.00	$2,387
Social science and medicine	$7.00	10	70.00	$1,680
totals		426	2,860.30	27,959.00

1994-95 for the top 20 journals, and their subscription cost for 1994. It's about ten cents on the dollar. These are the MOST heavily used titles. None of the other titles we bought articles from even came close to making us re-think owning them.

We have not, of course, just canceled this $446,000 worth of titles over the last decade. Our internal records show that as of June 1987, we had over 12,000 paid subscriptions. Today we have between 8,500 and 9,000 paid subscriptions. So we have been shedding titles on a large scale for most of this last decade. We aren't down that 8%, it is more like 25% for us. But even at this level, it is not enough to restore any kind of purchasing balance to our library materials budget. We are down from about 40,000 monographs a year to the 10 to 15 thousand level purchased in the same decade. And we are buying books this year because the university administration has provided us with one-time funds.

I would like to stress that this situation is NOT the result of cuts to the library budget. It is purely and simply a sign of the ravages of a serials system out of control on what in other times and climes would be considered a fairly reasonable chunk of change with which to buy library materials. And LSU, and to a lesser extent, other academic libraries in North America, have to figure out how to provide faculty and researchers what they need at a reasonable cost. We have had the luxury of pretty much ignoring that particular burden for a long time. It is a luxury we cannot continue to indulge.

I do have a practical problem, one many of you would enjoy I'm sure. As a result of our cancellation in 1995, we have a few extra dollars to add new subscriptions. It may be a first; in a year of 15% inflation, we are going to add new subscriptions. Since the faculty have identified 954 titles they want, all it would take would be a paltry $190,000 to meet their wishes. We have targeted about $50,000 for new subscriptions, for the areas we have surveyed.

It turns out that on a sheer numbers basis, that is if you just do it by the numbers and buy the titles where the largest number of faculty have landed, we would add about 40 titles, and they would be exclusively in physics and math. The faculty in those departments (12 of 94 in physics, and 22 of 44 in math) are very concentrated or at least in agreement on what are the most important new titles for their fields. And their numbers of agreement (11 of the 22 physics faculty agreed on a couple of titles) are higher than in any other departments. And they are higher than any combined totals for just about any other titles. We believe in a democracy, right, one man one vote, so why not?

As you look closely at the new journals requests a number of patterns come through very clearly. First, there are many departments where only one or two faculty are the experts in a particular field. And in some departments, none of the faculty cross anyone else, either in their department or on campus, in title needs. For instance, for the head of our federally funded Center for Advanced Micro Structure Devices (known locally as CAMD) there is one title that is supreme. *Molecular Crystals and Liquid Crystals.* Last time I checked that was over $17,000. As a manager, now, of limited resources, and not as some kind of collections guru, I know, from our data, that no title in that price range is going to be used enough to warrant that kind of price. In fact, from our data, again, the most cost-efficient title for the library to own is the cheaper title. It is more cost efficient to own a $50 title that 4 articles are needed from, than to own a $1,500 title that 100 articles are need from. It is more cost effective, under a document delivery or buy as needed model, to have the cheaper title in-house. Isn't that amazing, and isn't it exactly the opposite of what libraries have been doing. We have historically cancelled the cheaper titles to keep the more "important" titles in-house. And as a result, because we have been an inelastic market for those more expensive titles, just as any good economist would predict, the prices went up much faster than inflation, production, or any other cost would justify. The producers charged what the market would bear, and we and they have learned that is a great deal.

So for my ideal new subscription list I would add the cheapest titles wanted first. Secondly, we learned a very interesting fact. For the last decade, titles in QC class that had been mostly cut from our collection were the weather and climate titles. The constituency in physics has retired or been replaced over the last decade, and no single department had a critical mass of faculty looking out for climatology journals. But climate journal requests popped up all over our request lists, from every single college. There are climatologists in our coastal studies programs, in our agriculture programs, in geography, in engineering. But they are an invisible group because they are spread all over the university. And in no single department do they have enough presence to have protected those journals. They aren't expensive, as science titles go, but when pushed, the departmental process we've used to review them did not insure their survivability.

From this and similar observations in terms of titles requested, I determined to give first priority for new titles, not to the titles with the "most" votes, but to titles that were represented by the largest number of requests in terms of departments. And that became the primary method we used for determining the "big" dollar cost journals to be added. We wanted to protect and encourage interdisciplinarity FIRST. And although there were few titles that met this criteria, we added about 23 journals that cost about $20,000 that clearly were supported, often by very few individuals in any one department. That is, they were not "highly" ranked by any department at all.

Secondly, based on our experience with document delivery, i.e., the cheaper it is, the more cost effective it is to own, we looked for titles that fit our basic subject criteria, and used a base figure, in our case $75, as a multiplier. Each faculty request = $75. And if a title costs $750, then if 10 or more faculty wanted it, we added it to the list. Also, any title costing less than $75 with only one faculty requesting it, went into the purchase pile. If it met other more subjective criteria, it was added.

This is not a traditional way of adding new subscriptions. I think given the twin goals of interdisciplinary support and cost-effectiveness, it actually created a surprisingly diverse list. In all we are adding about 242 new journals, at a cost of $42,000. We could have added 40, and met the expressed needs of two departments. I am not holding this up as the prime example for deciding how to add new subscriptions. What I am doing is suggesting that the old ways of doing things have gotten us in the sorry state we are in, captive to producers who think nothing of pushing prices to us at triple and quadruple the inflation rate. It is time to change.

But it is not just in the arena of paper subscriptions that we must change. We have to change our perspective on what it is we do in libraries. We like to please those we consider our patrons. But we are now challenged to make cost-effective decisions that a few years ago would have sounded like heresy.

Before I close, I have one more observation from the data we collected. Although faculty noted that access was reasonable for 20% to 25% of the titles they identified, for a few departments the numbers were much different. For Biological and Agricultural Engineering, the faculty identified 9 new titles they wanted for subscriptions, and 28 they wanted as access. For Dairy Science, the figures were 12 subscription and 23 access, almost 2 to 1 for access. For Food Science, 5 subscription, 15 access. And for Human Ecology, 51 access and 46 subscription. These departments were so different from the rest of the responses, that I want to now what is going on. Why are they more ready than anyone else we've surveyed, to move to access for the titles they are interested in? I tend to think that as access becomes easier, more widespread, and the varieties of access increase, these numbers will increase in other departments and disciplines as well. But at the moment, on the LSU campus, clearly many of the departments in the College of Agriculture are moving quickly to accommodate, even welcome, a new environment.

Will Electronic Information Finally Result in Real Resource Sharing?

Frederick C. Lynden

INTRODUCTION

There are a hundred different scenarios for the future of libraries and more of them turn up every day. Suffice it to say that libraries are in turmoil, transition, and/or trouble. It is important to begin by speaking about predictions for the next millennium since there are now only four years until the second millennium is reached. Since it is difficult to be a seer, the quotations will come from others more farseeing:

> It is no longer a surrealistic fancy to see hundreds of millions of students, readers, professionals, researchers sitting in their private rooms or offices with their equipment, linked up to an encompassing and sophisticated system which will feed and project onto a screen any book, any article, any document. It will take one button pressed, one code impressed. And whatever one wants to look at or read will appear in its full panoply, down to the minutest detail. Every home, every office, every individual will be an automatic extension of the next century's

---

Frederick C. Lynden is Associate University Librarian for Technical Services at Brown University in Providence, RI.

[Haworth co-indexing entry note]: "Will Electronic Information Finally Result in Real Resource Sharing?" Lynden, Frederick C. Co-published simultaneously in *Journal of Library Administration* (The Haworth Press, Inc.) Vol. 24, No. 1/2, 1996, pp. 47-72; and: *Emerging Patterns of Collection Development in Expanding Resource Sharing, Electronic Information and Network Environment* (ed: Sul H. Lee) The Haworth Press, Inc., 1996, pp. 47-72. Single or multiple copies of this article are available for a fee from The Haworth Document Delivery Service [1-800-342-9678, 9:00 a.m. - 5:00 p.m. (EST). E-mail address: getinfo@haworth.com].

© 1996 by The Haworth Press, Inc. All rights reserved.

"Library of World Congress" or "Bibliotheque Internationale." (Talat S. Halman, NYU Professor of Near Eastern Laws and Literature)[1]

The printing press, the radio, television. And now emerges a new mutant technology which will combine and surpass all of these. It will enable five billion very individual human beings to have a single congruent view of human nature and existence. Able to live in Seattle and work in Singapore. Able to spend three thousand dollars and have access to 90% of the accumulated knowledge of humanity. (Steven Barnes, writer)[2]

The last forecast doesn't mention libraries, but one assumes that access to knowledge will somehow include libraries which will organize the accumulated knowledge.

Libraries must meet these challenges of the future. Another article in a futuristic issue of *ITEL*, called "The Information Future, Data, Data Everywhere,"[3] intentionally reminds one of a line in the "Ancient Mariner," "Water water everywhere, nor any drop to drink." Libraries are adapting very rapidly to the information age, but the infrastructure required makes it harder and harder to get that data. Access is much improved, but accessing data electronically increasingly requires more and more sophisticated software and hardware. And, at the same time and with the same resources, libraries are being asked to continue their twentieth-century role, i.e., building collections of books and journals and other types of library materials. Thus, the dilemma is one of obtaining resources for this transition.

Librarians are well aware of the current economic dilemma for research libraries. In the first place, universities are not able to support the library as well as in the past. University administrations are buffeted by countless challenges, among them competition for students, the costs of deferred maintenance, and expectations for advanced computer technology and telecommunications. A recent article in *Barron's* was entitled, "Campus Unrest, why parents are up in arms about tuition bills, and colleges will finally be forced to change their free-spending ways" (Jonathan R. Laing).[4] Second, there has been a decline in available federal monies as well as monies from other funding sources. The funding sources beyond the university are drying up because of the fierce competition for them as well as the greater accountability required. Taxpayers want to know how their money is spent and stockholders want an accounting of profits. Third, libraries have witnessed an inexorable rise in the costs of library materials. This problem has been demonstrated in innumerable ways, but the problem is basically a dilemma driven by the double-digit inflation of scholarly journals with the added surcharge of foreign currency exchange. As everyone knows, major scientific serials are now being published by multi-national corporations which have a strong hold, some say monopoly, on scientific information and have charged what the market will bear. Now the publishers are seeing numerous cancellations which have resulted in driving prices even higher. Fourth, libraries are no longer just purchasing books and journals but are required to buy many new media such as compact discs, CD-ROM's, and computer diskettes. Finally, libraries are running out of space at a time when the cost of building and real estate is also out of sight.

It is in the above context that library budgets are submitted. Over the past fifteen to twenty years at Brown University, it has been the custom for the Library to submit its budget to the Advisory Committee on University Planning (ACUP) which looks at budgets from all parts of the campus. The ACUP group includes the Provost, other administration officials, professors, and students. This group critically examines the proposals of various departments and then makes recommendations which take into account the competitive requests of units on the campus and attempts to prioritize their needs. In fiscal 1997, the cost of a Brown education for one year will be $28,796 with $21,712 of this being allocated to tuition. The principal areas for increase are costs of faculty and staff raises, higher fringe benefit costs, student aid increases and rising operating expenditures including debt service. In fiscal 1997, the overall budget will be increased by 4.7 percent. One looks in vain for mention of the Library in this budget. Of course, the Library always submits a separate figure for the increase in its library materials budget and this request has been at a double-digit level for eight of the past ten years. In January 1994, when ACUP made its recommendations for the 1994/95 budget, the following was stated:

Library Acquisitions: ACUP recommends adding $130,000 for library books and periodicals. While the Committee recognizes this is not enough to keep pace with inflation, it also acknowledges the futility of matching annual double digit inflationary increases for books and periodicals. ACUP supports all efforts to enhance access to library materials through non-traditional means such as electronic services and intercollegiate sharing.[5]

This approach was a new direction for ACUP and signaled the end of their attempts to meet the Library's requests for materials budget increases at a double-digit level. Incidentally, the increase for 96/97 library materials budget (now over $4 million) will be 9%, but this increase includes a 7.5% increase from the President's contingency funds which will not be added to the base. One suspects that the above scenario is not very different for libraries at other university campuses throughout the United States. In other words, university administrations, despite their good intentions, are no longer able to meet the demands for increasing library materials budgets at double-digit levels. Although there may be an occasional increase at that level, it is no longer possible to sustain regular increases at double-digit level.

ELECTRONIC SERVICES

In general, "electronic services" describe the variety of electronic media which a modern research university library must support. For example, most university libraries have an on-line public access catalog (OPAC). Frequently, the OPAC also provides electronic access to acquisitions, serials, circulation, and reserves. In addition, libraries subscribe to the services of bibliographic utilities such as RLG and OCLC. These utilities allow libraries to view the holdings of other libraries and facilitate interlibrary loan. In addition, libraries purchase access to a variety of databases providing indexing and abstracting services in all subjects. Further, libraries usually provide a gateway to the Internet and its World Wide Web services as well as the gophers from many campuses. Libraries also hook into the local campus network in order to provide electronic communication through e-mail and to offer software for word processing, spreadsheets, and other information management programs. These new electronic services, many of which did not exist ten years ago, now are demanded by faculty and students alike. In 1993/94 the Brown University Library spent more than nine percent of its *entire* budget on electronic services. In 1994/95, the Brown University Library spent more than four percent of its *materials budget* on electronic services (not including document delivery) whereas it is estimated that OCLC libraries are now spending 8-14% of their materials budgets on electronic information, including document delivery.[6]

Unfortunately, the intention of ACUP, when this group spoke about enhancing Brown's access to materials through electronic services, was to increase access without increasing costs. In other words, the university proposed to transfer the costs from journal subscriptions to electronic document delivery. Most of the advocates of virtual or digital libraries tend to view the adoption of electronic services as an antidote to the inexorable rise in materials prices. Currently many libraries deal with high serial costs through cancellation and use of document delivery services. Charles Hamaker's report on Louisiana State University at Baton Rouge is a prime example.[7] There are many commercial document delivery services available now from such firms as CARL, EBSCO/doc, and University Microfilms International (UMI). These services offer delivery of articles by fax, express mail, or electronically. They sell articles to libraries or individuals. This type of service is an economy for the library because the library no longer has to purchase the periodical or serial title, but can obtain a copy of a portion of the contents. The article has become the unit.

Librarians are well aware of the many advantages to electronic information. First, there is often a general fee, which the university—not the library—pays, for services such as Internet. This fee, often paid by another party, the university, for example, is a real bargain in terms of the resources it purchases. Second, electronic information can be obtained from remote locations rapidly and without postage. Third, electronic sources are very economic in terms of time and flexibility. For example, electronic reference tools can be used remotely, searched by keyword, and can consolidate many years of physical volumes. A fourth advantage of using electronic sources is that the electronic text can be transferred electronically to a personal database. Finally, many argue that the electronic files are less expensive than print files because the costs for binding, storage, and retrieval are greatly reduced or eliminated.

Nevertheless, it is now widely conceded that there can be major costs and impediments to adopting electronic technology. First, observers see the supplemental costs of technology raising the overall costs of the library. Libraries must now own and operate expensive special equipment such as high-end computers, scanners such as ARIEL, and high speed printers. Furthermore, this equipment must be maintained and upgraded. Second, there are clearly staff costs to run, program, and maintain machinery, and to educate the users. It is clear that more skilled staff are required now to assist patrons in using electronic materials. Electronic reference tools have their own unique codes for searching fields, different operators for searching, different log-ins and exits, and different function keys. However, libraries have minimized the differences through the use of programming. Of course, this kind of expertise does not come inexpensively nor does the assistance necessarily come very rapidly. In addition to the staff expertise required to assist users, staff expertise and equipment are required for the processing of these materials. Third, the advantages to the user do not always translate into lower costs for the library. For example, it is true that, if the Library offers free printing, some computer searches especially among untrained users, bring large results and the number of pages printed can be daunting. According to Walt Crawford and Michael Gorman in *Future Libraries: Dreams, Madness, and Reality*, "a 'virtual' UCLA Library would produce as much paper *every year* as is now contained in the library and involve spending $160 on printing on demand for every $100 now spent on *all library collections, programs, and services*."[8] Costs are increased by printing, by the need for more high-end equipment for networking and downloading, as well as by receiving data from the World Wide Web with its color graphics.

There are also costs and impediments to using document delivery for access. First, the article databases have a copyright fee for all articles and, since the copyright fee is a sliding fee based upon the publisher's decision, it can reduce the cost advantage of document delivery. For example, the *Journal of Academic Librarianship* has a copyright fee of $50 per article used, but a subscription costs only $158 per annum.[9] Therefore, if a library requests more than three articles from this title, then it is more cost effective to purchase the journal. It is clear that publishers can and will use the copyright fee to recover costs or encourage libraries to purchase the title. Second, in some cases the copyright holder does not permit a document supplier to deliver. For example, an article by James H. Billington entitled the "Electronic Library," had this restriction: "The copyright holder of this article does not permit UnCover to deliver this item."[10] Third, there is no single document delivery source, and many times the library's principal document delivery service may not offer the title which the patron is seeking. Therefore, it is necessary to query several different sources in order to find the document. Again, software or human intervention can cut down on these problems, but these solutions are also costly.

Probably the most serious problem with electronic materials is that their costs tend to detract from the ability of the library to purchase other materials. Few libraries have been able to establish special funds for electronic materials, nor have additional funds been made available over and above the library materials budget. When a library has been able to establish a separate fund, it may mean fewer funds for other subjects. In short, electronic materials are supplemental to all of the other materials which the library purchases. Both Duane Webster and Mary Jackson warn:

> The access model, taken to its ultimate conclusion, could result in a single subscription to a journal title, but that is a scenario neither publishers nor librarians wish to see materialize. If libraries continue to reduce collection development to focus only on local and immediate needs, then the "commons" that scholars rely on will become impoverished. The access model will self-destruct.[11]

Another observer of this situation, Dennis Dickinson, College Librarian at Beloit College in Wisconsin notes:

> if libraries continue to draw down material budgets to fund technology, they risk putting in place highly efficient and

expensive mechanisms for sharing resources, while at the same time diminishing the very resources they hope to share. The inevitable result of this cost shifting . . . will be the expeditious pooling of poverty.[12]

These are warnings which librarians should heed, and one means of heeding them is to put into place effective resource sharing.

It is obvious that the previous methods of coping with an inability to obtain resources for the Library are becoming less effective. Libraries are not having as much success with their administrations in obtaining budgetary relief. They are still attaining their goals in fund raising, but the rate at which materials costs are inflating diminishes this success. As noted earlier, obtaining grants and gifts is becoming more difficult. Most libraries have canceled duplicates by now, and they are now cutting into their serial collections heavily with cancellations. Access rather than acquisition is a significant means of dealing with scarce resources but, as noted above, electronic access adds a supplementary cost and apparently it will always carry with it certain staffing, equipment, and maintenance costs which will never disappear. Resource sharing now appears to be one of the few remaining means of contending with shrinking budgets and the lack of financial resources. More and more libraries are joining consortia for the purpose of resource sharing. An announcement of a new collaboration was received January in 1996. Six research institutions in the Chesapeake Bay region have formed an alliance called the Chesapeake Information and Research Library Alliance (CIRLA). It is comprised of the University of Delaware, Georgetown University, Howard University, Johns Hopkins University, the University of Maryland at College Park, and the Smithsonian Institution. These institutions are all members of the Association of Research Libraries (ARL). Their stated goal is "to enhance education and research at member institutions through collaborative development of library collection and service programs and expanding use of information technology."[13] Economic conditions may be forcing libraries into resource sharing, but information technology improves the quality of that sharing. It is not surprising that libraries are seeking to employ resource sharing to obtain the results they cannot secure through other efforts. There is not only a long history of resource sharing, but the concept of using electronic networks to facilitate and improve library collaboration also has historical antecedents going back twenty-five years.

ELECTRONIC RESOURCE SHARING: A HISTORICAL PERSPECTIVE

Twenty-five years ago last fall the American Library Association and the U.S. Office of Education, Bureau of Libraries and Educational Technology held a conference on "Interlibrary Communications and Information Networks." There were 125 invited participants and the conference also received advice and assistance from seventeen professional organizations, among them the National Academy of Sciences and the National Science Foundation. "The aim was to explore and study the implications that would follow if a network of libraries and information centers were established in the United States . . . if maximum communication could be established among them, the resultant interconnection of resources would constitute a unique national information apparatus of immense value to the economic, cultural, and social growth of the country."[14] The Conference recommended that the "National Commission on Libraries and Information Science devise a comprehensive plan to facilitate the coordinated development of the nation's libraries, information centers, and other knowledge sources."[15] There were also working group recommendations which covered areas such as standard bibliographic data records for all forms of materials, financial support from legislative proposals at federal and state levels, interdisciplinary education training programs for librarians and information scientists, coordination with the Office of Telecommunications Policy and the FCC, coordination with other countries for international transfer of information, and policy development by the National Commission. These were recommendations ahead of their time.

Now, twenty-five years later, many of these recommendations are in place. Despite this progress, there are some gnawing problems which were also mentioned at the conference:

> First, there are a number of factors which limit self-sufficiency and require networking. These factors are financial, the information explosion, space, and unavailability of materials.

Second, libraries and information centers will need to become "pro-active" rather than reactive social institutions in order to prosecute network objectives forcefully.

Third, copyright is a major concern. A question was raised about documents in the computer: " . . . is the copyright law violated when a document is put into a computer data base or when it is displayed? . . . How, then should the process of modifying texts, manipulating them and consolidating their content, and displaying them in new ways be interpreted under the law?"

Fourth, compatibility of machine systems is also a concern. Mentioned were the difficulties of arriving at standards and formats that can be used for transfer of information.

Finally, a major concern is information access among "different constituencies, geographic regions, and groups.[16]

If these concerns sound familiar, they are still very much with us in today's new network environment.

The conference theme was interlibrary communications and information networks, so several of the papers dealt with interlibrary cooperation. One of the papers described the American Library Association's official policy statements as indicating that ALA believed that no one library or type of library could be self-sufficient. Further, it indicated that national legislation had provided funds under a 1968 amendment to the Higher Education Act of 1965, Title VIII, Networks for Knowledge, "to encourage colleges and universities to *share* to an optimal extent, through cooperative arrangements, their technical and other educational and administrative facilities and *resources* . . . "[17] Unfortunately, funds were not authorized for this Title. However, the concept of "resource sharing" was definitely imbedded in this legislation.

Another of the conference papers spoke about NPAC, the National Program for Acquisitions and Cataloging, a part of the Higher Education Act of 1965, which required the Library of Congress to acquire, on a comprehensive basis, currently published foreign scholarly material and to catalog it promptly. An adjunct to the NPAC program was the ARL program to send to LC notification of research titles received in ARL libraries which LC then cataloged. This paper also described the Association of Research Libraries Cooperative Acquisitions Project which obtained material from Europe during World War II and later became the Farmington Plan. This plan was a national coordinated collection plan whereby certain libraries had responsibility for collecting materials of specific countries.

Still another paper described the FAUL organization, the Five Associated University Libraries, SUNY Binghamton, SUNY Buffalo, Cornell University, Syracuse University, and the University of Rochester. In 1970, they collectively held 8 million volumes and total library expenditures were $13.2 million in fiscal 1969, about $1 million less than Harvard. In its constitution, the organization spoke of coordinated acquisitions policies, shared resources, development of compatible machine systems, provision of easy and rapid communication systems among the membership, the provision of shared storage facilities and exploration of other areas of cooperation. One of the projects was to share the purchase of particularly expensive items with no conditions placed on location but the requirement of a unit borrowing card for all libraries and the right to request the items on interlibrary loan.[18]

Although many of the above programs are moribund, the concepts for cooperation and sharing resources are very much alive. The problems which existed at that time have also persisted to the present. However, there are now more sophisticated solutions to these problems. For example, there are now standards for interchange of information from computer system to computer system and compatibility is not as serious a problem. Nevertheless, political and financial issues relating to compatibility remain. They will be discussed in this paper.

RESOURCE SHARING TODAY

Any definition of resource sharing should probably begin with the *ALA Glossary* of 1983 which described resource sharing as:

> A term covering a variety of organizations and activities engaged in jointly by a group of libraries for the purposes of improving services and/or cutting costs. Resource sharing may

be established by informal or formal agreement or by contract and may operate locally, nationally, or internationally. The resources shared may be collections, bibliographic data, personnel, planning activities, etc. Formal organizations for resource sharing may be called bibliographic utilities, cooperative systems, consortia, networks, bibliographic service centers, etc.[19]

Of course, in the electronic era, there are many other activities which can be subsumed under the expression "resource sharing." For example, sharing of electronic resources, consortial site licenses, and shared computer storage will be more commonplace. Resource sharing has many facets in the collection arena. Following is a list of the types of resource sharing which can impact collection building.

First, *coordinated collection development* is an extremely effective type of resource sharing. It has been done in North Carolina since the 1930s. Three libraries, the so-called Research Triangle libraries, University of North Carolina-Chapel Hill, Duke, and North Carolina State participate in this endeavor. The libraries have cooperated in area studies, dividing collecting geographically for Latin American countries, Slavic and East European, African, and Asian. The cooperative has included the University of Virginia which has participated in the Slavic and East European area collecting, and Tulane University which has participated in Latin American area acquisitions. Collecting has also been divided along lines of unique academic strengths, e.g., Duke in Forestry and Oriental history and UNC in geology and library science. Another area is the collection of depository documents, dividing by various international agencies. The institutions have also coordinated the purchases of microform sets.

Second, *collaborative collection development* has occurred at the U.C. system and at Stanford. This type of collection development depends upon a pool of monies shared by ten University of California institutions and Stanford which is then used to purchase materials. A recent account of the Science Translation Journal Pilot Project explains that this project provides shared access to translation journals in the physical sciences and saves the libraries more than $100,000 a year.[20] This project is one of many in which these ten institutions have engaged. The Shared Acquisitions effort is called Shared Collections and Access Program or SCAP. There is a central pot of money amounting to about 3% of the total acquisition budgets of the UC libraries. From this fund, the libraries have acquired millions of dollars worth of materials while avoiding duplication of these materials.

Third, *consortial cost sharing* rather than pooling monies uses cooperation to obtain discounts for materials. Cost sharing is allowing libraries to finance electronic acquisitions. The *Chronicle of Higher Education* reports that "more institutions are turning to library consortia as a way to combine their purchasing power and win better deals on everything from the electronic version of *Encyclopaedia Brittanica* to data bases of poetry and scientific abstracts."[21] Several examples are noted from TexShare, representing 52 libraries at medical centers and public, four year colleges, to VIVA in Virginia and GALILEO in Georgia. According to Joseph J. Esposito, President of Brittanica, the selling of Brittanica products to consortia is a "win-win situation for the consortium and the vendor."

Fourth, *cooperative holdings agreements* are another form of resource sharing which relies on conspectuses from a consortium. The Boston Library Consortium (BLC), which includes sixteen academic, research, and special libraries, among them five ARL institutions: Boston Public Library, University of Massachusetts at Amherst, Boston University, Massachusetts Institute of Technology (MIT) and Brown (which joined in 1996), has made several cooperative holdings agreements. For example, the Cooperative Holding of Chemistry Journal Titles Agreement assigns titles to certain institutions who then agree to serve as "primary provider" to other libraries.[22] The Consortium will regularly review agreements and they will fully honor copyright obligations. Further, BLC has just begun its own delivery system using a commercial service which has a van.

Fifth, *consortial sharing of electronic resources* is another important type of resource sharing to enhance collections. The Committee on Interinstitutional Cooperation (CIC), the Big Ten universities and the University of Chicago have recently begun an effort to jointly produce and distribute electronic texts in the Humanities.[23] Not only will this collaboration provide networked access to sources within CIC libraries, but it will also set up procedures for adding new resources. Further, it will provide a model for text search and retrieval as well as shared expertise. In the end, there will be seamless access to all CIC electronic resources in the Humanities. Duplication of costly individual library efforts will be avoided and will increase the resources available to each library.

Another example of shared electronic resources comes from a member of OhioLINK, Wright State. Arnold Hirschon reports that by the end of 1994, "OhioLINK databases eliminated the local need for 15 out of 23 disks."[24] These databases are centrally funded, and are obtained at a lower cost through centralized buying. Further, these databases are maintained on high level machines with excellent response time and almost unlimited access. Individual institutions do not have to pay for the databases or for access to them.

The sixth and most widespread form of resource sharing is *common interlibrary loan*. This form of cooperation clearly extends the collections. Most commonly, libraries locate materials using bibliographic utilities. OCLC now has holdings symbols for over 500 million items and its ILL volume is now over 8 million requests per annum. Further, OCLC now has an ILL Fee Management service which tracks interlibrary loan charges, and consequently reduces ILL overhead.[25] RLG, with over 73 million records, has introduced ARIEL which is an electronic full-text transmission software having advantages of clarity, speed, and cost over fax. In the future, ARIEL will be transmittable via electronic mail in its MIME (Multipurpose Internet Mail Extensions) version.[26]

Many libraries now avoid paying any fees through cooperative interlibrary loan agreements. One such resource sharing/interlibrary loan program is that of the CIC (Big Ten plus Chicago). Within this group there are free interlibrary loans and photocopies and most libraries had agreed to no limitations on format as of 1989.[27] Turnaround time and delivery have been improved through the use of fax, ARIEL, and UPS.

A seventh form of resource sharing is *cooperative or shared storage*. Storage is an important consideration in collection management since collection funds can be consumed by storage costs. A cooperative storage facility can assist libraries through a last copy policy. In other words, all but one copy of a duplicated title can be held at the storage facility saving costs for all parties. The Center for Research Libraries is clearly the best example of this type of storage. In existence since 1951, when it was the Midwest Interlibrary Center, the Center for Research Libraries has developed a number of innovative cooperative programs, including the microfilming of foreign newspapers. The Center administers five cooperative area studies microform projects: the Cooperative Africana Microform Project (CAMP), the Latin American Microform Project (LAMP), the Middle East Microform Project (MEMP), the South Asia Microform Project (SAMP), and the Southeast Asia Microform Project (SEAM). The Center is now embarking on a capital campaign to modernize and expand its facilities. They have received a $575,000 Challenge Grant from NEH.[28] The University of California Northern Regional Facility is another example of a cooperative effort. This storage facility began in 1983 with 2 million volumes from four universities. The facility is managed by the Northern Regional Library Board which consists of directors from the contributing institutions, a faculty representative from each, and the state librarian.[29] Most storage facilities have staff on site to provide for delivery of materials either via van or in the case of articles by fax or electronic means, e.g., ARIEL.

Eighth, *cooperative education and expertise* are part of resource-sharing agreements. VIVA, the Virtual Library of Virginia, a program set up in 1994, has established regional electronic resource centers which will provide full-text information in electronic format. "The six regional centers will divide responsibilities among themselves to maximize the development and use of local expertise."[30] For sharing in a virtual library environment, there will be different divisions, i.e., other than geographic or by discipline. These will include division by "type of software needed, sharing of network load, or distribution by ability to provide reference assistance."[31] VIVA has received $5.2 million from the state for electronic collections, equipment for resource centers, for workstations in all 51 libraries, training in the use of electronic collections, support for expediting interlibrary loan, software for linking systems and patron ILL, and resource-sharing training.

Ninth, *common or linked online systems* are an essential part of collection resource sharing. In Louisiana, LOUIS, or the Louisiana Online University Information System, was established in 1993. This system was made possible by a $2.48 million grant from the federal government. LOUIS is a NOTIS-based electronic network connecting the OPAC's of the Louisiana academic libraries. Based on this network, LALINC, or the Louisiana Academic Library Information Network Consortium, will now be able to consider cooperative projects.[32] In 1992, the research libraries of Michigan (University of Michigan, Wayne State, and Michigan State) formed a research triangle and the libraries expect to connect via M-Link, the University of Michigan's telecommunications network.[33] In Florida, community colleges have now linked up with the state universities to share resources, ILL, and e-mail. In 1993, it was announced that LINCC (Library Information Network for Community Colleges), connecting 28 community colleges, hooked up with FIRN (Florida Information Resources Network) to permit access to each other and to electronic databases.[34] These are a few of the statewide efforts.

Tenth, *cooperative delivery systems* are an essential part of the resource-sharing movement. Delivery of the document to the user is the *raison d'être* of resource sharing. An example of cooperative delivery effort involving University of Oklahoma is the Greater Midwest Research Library Consortium (GMRLC) which, as of 1995, has invested in an interstate courier system to deliver materials to GMRLC libraries.[35] The Boston Library Consortium also began a delivery system in 1996.[36] In the electronic age, delivery can also mean receiving full text online. An example of this type of cooperative plan is the recent agreement between RLG, PICA (the Dutch Centre for Library Automation), and Kluwer. According to a recent press release:

> The new service will allow endusers to search WebCAT, a special catalog of bibliographic records (maintained in parallel on both the RLG and Pica host computers, via Web browsers and to retrieve documents linked to them—full text, articles, maps, images, etc.—using Web technology. WebDOC interposes a licensing and accounting server between the catalog record and access to the whole document it describes, to verify

that the user is covered by an institutional license or else to debit the user's personal account.[37]

This is a cooperative variation of the commercial document delivery system which has become a very significant part of the "access versus acquisition" paradigm.

Real Resource Sharing

Many of the above examples provide clues to what real resource sharing is. Real resource sharing should have the following characteristics:

1. *Requirements of users* are most often *satisfied* in a real resource-sharing situation. An excellent example of an effective plan is the *Research Triangle* sharing where libraries are coordinating resources so that the user can obtain materials rapidly.
2. Materials are *ready when the user needs them* in a real resource-sharing situation. Examples of document delivery systems are noted above.
3. Materials are *readily available* when the user is looking for them in a real resource-sharing environment. Many of the cooperative online catalogs provide this possibility. An example given earlier is the LOUIS network in Louisiana.
4. Real resource sharing *realizes savings*. An example of this type of benefit is the discounts offered by TexShare in group purchases.
5. Real resource sharing *reduces costs*. With all libraries contributing to a joint purchase each library pays less. An excellent example of this is the Stanford/UC resource-sharing cooperation.
6. *Resources* are *increased locally* in a successful resource-sharing plan. In the Boston Library Consortium there are 16 institutions with a combined collection of over 23 million volumes.
7. *Resources* are *shared nationally* in a successful resource-sharing plan. At the Center for Research Libraries, a cooperative storage library, foreign newspapers, among other materials, are collected and filmed, and the membership of CRL is national in composition.

8. *Resources* of a *monetary nature* can be *procured* for the partners in an effective resource-sharing plan. An example is VIVA, which obtained $5.2 million from the state of Virginia for their virtual library experiments.
9. *Retention agreements* are kept in an effective resource-sharing plan. The cooperative holdings agreements at the BLC are examples of decisions made by consortium members to ensure that there are always holdings of a title.
10. A successful resource-sharing plan *remains in place* because it is supported by top administrative officials and looks beyond immediate needs through developing a common understanding of the purposes of the project. At VIVA, there was always involvement of the project directors and a high degree of mutual trust developed by the directors.

Recent Expansion of Resource Sharing

There is evidence of increased resource sharing as librarians have realized that the new electronic access model results in incremental costs. William Miller at Florida Atlantic writes about the Internet:

> Isn't information free on the Internet? The answer unfortunately is: "In the long run you get what you pay for." Interesting bits of data are currently available on the Internet, but the creators have no obligation to continue to provide them. Users have no right to insist on their availability. And quality and timeliness are both conspicuously absent in much of this information.[38]

He goes on to speak about the frequent necessity of paying for both the online and paper versions of a title. Libraries often pay per use or number of users rather than having a paper document which can be used by any number of readers. Another problem is that publishers don't necessarily have any commitment to keep copies in perpetuity. Each of these tradeoffs has a cost. One publisher, Charles Germain, has also recently commented on librarians' misconceptions about the electronic world. He notes the following misconceptions:

misconception 1: Access to articles is going to be cheaper than ownership of journals.

misconception 2: Electronic storage is much more cost effective than shelf space.
misconception 3: Paper is expensive.
misconception 4: Vendors and publishers are going to be the conservators.
misconception 5: Research and development costs for entry into new media are manageable.[39]

Here are some recent examples of resource-sharing agreements or expansions: the Research Triangle University Libraries added another library, North Carolina Central University, to its group in 1995, raising its total to 4. The Boston Library Consortium added Brown University in 1996 to its 15 member consortium raising the total to 16. In 1992, Michigan libraries formed their research triangle with University of Michigan, Wayne State, and Michigan State. In 1993, the Louisiana Online University Information Center was founded. CIRLA, the Chesapeake Information and Research Library Alliance, including ARL libraries from the District of Columbia area, was formed in 1996. VIVA, the Virginia Virtual Library, was proposed in 1993 and funded in 1994. In 1992, the libraries of the University of California and Stanford University began to offer reciprocal borrowing privileges. Together the resources of these institutions amount to 28.8 million volumes. Although the Five Associated University Libraries (FAUL) no longer exists, the eleven research libraries in NY State (NY State Library, the 4 SUNY libraries, Syracuse, Cornell, Columbia, NYU, NYPL, and Rochester) that applied in the early 90s for preservation funds from the state of New York were successful and there is a cooperative pooled fund for preservation. These examples are obviously not complete, but they do demonstrate a resurgence of interest and activities related to resource sharing in the 90s. They represent a national spectrum of activities, and indicate a revival of shared activities aimed at increasing access to resources. Arnold Hirschon has speculated that this increase in resource sharing is due to four factors: economic tightening; quality improvement (i.e., more accountability requiring reduction of operating costs); expanding information; and the growth of information technology.[40] There is a report from the Boston Library Consortium that "in the decade between 1983 and 1993, the BLC's libraries' lending activity grew by 80% and borrowing activity by 89%."[41]

CONCLUSION

There are many ways in which resource sharing can help blunt the impact of the incremental costs of the electronic delivery of information. In this transitional period, the library community is being asked to develop these new electronic resources at the same time it is being told that these new resources should reduce the costs of service and the need to purchase locally by permitting access beyond the local collection. It is true that the new electronic resources provide immediate and wide-ranging information bases that allow patrons to range worldwide in doing their research, and resources no longer have to be local. But there is a danger that by exchanging dollars, once destined for collections, for electronic resources and equipment, that the local collections will begin to wither and there will be a poverty of the whole. Below are some recommendations which aim at improving resource sharing and lessening the impact of these new factors.

First, efforts made by ARL and AAU to return to collection coordination through a national system of collection building should continue. The Farmington Plan was a post-war experiment to develop a system of collecting which would include every country in the world and assign a library to collect each country's publications. It was as much a measure of national defense as an effort to understand other cultures. For whatever reason, it seems logical to consider adopting some plan of national coordination again. At least three countries have mounted a similar effort. England has a model plan with its National Central Lending Library where serials are collected and can be shared by the entire country. In Australia, there are efforts underway to develop a "Distributed National Collection" (DNC) based upon conspectuses produced in Australian libraries. In Germany, there is a series of special libraries, e.g., one for engineering, another for agriculture, another for economic sciences, and another for medicine. In the United States, the medical library system provides a good example of collection coordination which is automated.

Second, ARL should coordinate information from regional or statewide groupings of libraries. For example, ARL could, with the help of the Council on Library Resources (CLR), establish a clearinghouse of activities and keep track of last copy titles to insure that there would be a last copy of a serial title somewhere in the United States. In cooperation with the Library of Congress, ARL could provide a union catalog (or database) of serial last copies in this country. The Library of Congess has prepared catalogs for Microform Masters and Manuscripts. There are certainly other activities ARL could coordinate in area studies, special formats, and/or electronic resources.

Third, with national leadership from ARL or LC, libraries could coordinate the collecting in the existing remote storage facilities, and operate in the manner of the Center for Research Libraries. There may already be nascent developments along these lines. For example, the Boston Library Consortium is considering the possibility of a shared storage facility. This facility would include such activities as shared cost of maintaining space and delivery services, development of collective or joint ownership for some classes of materials, inclusion of materials jointly purchased by the Consortium, and provision of such specialized services as a preservation lab or secured areas for rare or valuable materials.

Fourth, libraries will need to develop common site licenses and delivery services as have the Research Libraries Group and PICA. The PICA network and its WebDOC system is the first cooperative system on the network which has developed document maintenance and accounting procedures. Their system ensures that the documents are available, and indexed. There is available at PICA (the Dutch Centre for Library Automation) a shared cataloging and document-ordering system. This Centre has also made arrangements with publishers to provide their documents. Publishers can rely on the security of this system, i.e., insuring against unauthorized use and receiving their payments.

Fifth, there needs to be more cooperative effort toward cataloging the Internet. OCLC has developed one plan to catalog the Internet. OCLC received $62,000 from the U.S. Education Department and added $45,327 of its own funds to assemble a catalog of Internet Accessible Resources.[42] OCLC asked for librarians and other

Internet users to assist in this project. Again, however, participation from ARL and LC is needed in order to ensure that standards are developed and coordination occurs. A program along the lines of NACO should be developed. Such a program would also authenticate the sources of information since one of the major problems of the Internet is the lack of any authoritative verification of sources on it. Another serious problem is indexing which articles are available through delivery services. Perhaps CLR can fund an effort to develop an umbrella index for document delivery services.

Sixth, electronic data cannot begin to replace paper as a medium until there is more full-text data. Clearly, the efforts by LC to establish a Digital Library and projects such as J-STOR (the Andrew Mellon Foundation Project to convert into electronic form pre-1990 issues of ten core scholarly journals in the fields of Economics and History) are promising. The J-STOR project focused on back issues for three reasons: (a) these titles were in need of preservation; (b) they were not readily accessible; and (c) they used up so much stack space. This area of retrospective conversion, i.e., retrospective conversion of journals into full text, seems a very promising area for resource-sharing consortia if there is some coordination by a body such as ARL or LC. Such work would ensure electronic archival copies. However, even the J-STOR project suggested "arrangements . . . for regional collections of paper copies."[43] Nevertheless, this is an area for coordinated resource sharing. Once these data are available, there should be a central database maintained to avoid duplication of efforts.

Seventh, another area where concerted and coordinated action should be taken is the reporting of detailed holdings. Observers see incomplete or missing serials holding data as a major obstacle to effective sharing of resources. The medical library community is setting a very good example for other libraries:

> Perhaps the best example of cooperative control of serials is DOC-LINE, the NLM-automated ILL system for medical libraries, where 80% of the contributing libraries report specific serial holdings. Because of this high level of participation, DOC-LINE boasts an impressive ILL fill rate of 92% to 99%; the majority of requests are satisfied on the first or second location.[44]

The advantage of holdings data is that libraries can view holdings of "specialized, esoteric, rare or foreign publications" in online union lists while, at the same time, requesting the more common titles via document delivery services. In the long run, online detailed holdings of uncommon titles will also be linked to delivery mechanisms. In any case, the efforts to improve holdings data can perhaps best be done through a shared effort.

Eighth, consortia have experimented with user-initiated interlibrary loan and this mode of seeking holdings is proving to be very efficient. "Online borrowing relies upon the patron to verify the item to borrow, select the lending institution, and place the request." At OhioLINK a study showed that once patron-initiated borrowing was feasible, the traffic through ILL lessened.[45] Further, the OhioLINK system is offered free of charge to users. At the moment, articles must still be ordered through ILL, and OhioLINK is making an effort to develop patron-initiated loans for articles, as well as encouraging the use of commercial suppliers.

Ninth, more libraries need to consider the possibilities of consortial purchasing. Not only are there advantages to this type of purchasing in terms of discounts, but there are also distinct benefits from the cost avoidance viewpoint. Not only will large sets or significant databases be purchased in this manner, but also hardware and software will be obtained in this manner. When it is not possible to get agreement on equipment or titles, it may be possible to achieve improved purchasing power and choice through overlapping consortia. Libraries are already taking advantage of such overlap. For example, Brown University Library can obtain discounts on equipment and some databases through NELINET while it also intends to work through the Boston Library Consortium for other materials.

Tenth, in the long range it will be important for libraries to study how best to take advantage of resource sharing, not only to look at its dynamics. For example, the experience of the Research Triangle Libraries in North Carolina shows the importance of administrative agreement, adequate funding, a vision and commitment to sharing, formal structures, recognition by operating staff of the importance of sharing, shared holdings information, and a willingness to maximize the availability of collections.[46] Further, there needs to be high level participation, mutual trust, a willingness to experiment, and a commitment to continued involvement. The Boston Library Consortium felt it important enough to invite ARL consultants to BLC to insure the success of its development of cooperative collection development programs. The consultants worked with 28 staff and 8 directors of member libraries for two days in 1993.

> The institute was designed to provide participants an opportunity to explore key questions concerning resource sharing and to engage in experiences that would enhance their understanding of the strategies and skills necessary to make resource sharing successful.[47]

This type of commitment to the process is necessary to make resource sharing successful.

In summary, technology has enabled libraries to improve on resource sharing. As has been noted at this conference, it is now possible to connect worldwide. Technology has also made it possible for the user to initiate his or her own interlibrary loan and this has facilitated delivery. However, in the end, it is the personal and political issues, as always, which determine whether or not resource sharing will succeed. Real resource sharing demands shared values, vision, and commitment, as well as a good political situation, special funding, and full participation by all staff.

ENDNOTES

1. Halman, Talat S. "From Babylon to Librespace." *IFLA Journal* 21:257 (1995).
2. Barnes, Steven. "The Impossible Dream." *Information Technology and Libraries* 14:268 (December 1995).
3. Wolf, Milton T. and R. Bruce Miller. "The Information Future: Data Data Everywhere." *Information Technology and Libraries* 14:215 (December 1995).
4. Laing, Jonathan R. "Campus Unrest." *Barron's* LXXV:25 (27 November 1995).
5. Advisory Committee on University Planning. "Special Report: Budget Recommendations for 1994-95." *George Street Journal* 18:7 (February 16, 1994).
6. Dillon, Leslie. "Notes on the November 6-7, 1995 Meeting." *Memorandum of January 2, 1996 to the Research Libraries Advisory Committee.* p. 3.

7. Hayes, John R. "The Internet's First Victim?" *Forbes* 156:201 (December 18, 1995).

8. Crawford, Walter and Michael Gorman. *Future Libraries: Dreams, Madness, and Reality.* Chicago and London American Library Association, 1995. p. 143.

9. Swindler, Luke. "From the Mailbox." *Newsletter On Serials Pricing Issues* 155.4 (February 16,1996)

10. James H. Billinton, "The Electronic Library." *Media studies journal* 8:109 (Winter 1994). Cited in UnCover.

11. Webster, Duane E. and Mary E. Jackson. "Key Issue: The Peril and Promise of Access." *Journal of Academic Librarianship* 20:261 (November 1994).

12. Dickinson, Dennis. "Academic Libraries on the Cusp." *Library Issues* 15:1 (January 1995).

13. Neal, James, "Chesapeake Information and Research Library Alliance (CIRLA) formed by six ARL institutions," *Press Release* John Hopkins Library, March 18, 1996.

14. Becker, Joseph, ed. *Proceedings of the Conference on Interlibrary Communications and Information Networks.* Chicago: American Library Association, 1971, p1.

15. *Ibid.*, 5.

16. *Ibid.*, 57, 4, 25, 24, and 5.

17. *Ibid.*, 44-45.

18. *Ibid.*, 266-276.

19. Heartsill, Young. "Resource Sharing." *The ALA Glossary of Library and Information Science.* Chicago: ALA, 1983, p. 194.

20. Hightower, Christie and George Soete. "The Consortium as Learning Organization: Twelve Steps to Success in Collaborative Collections Projects." *Journal of Academic Librarianship.* 21:87 (March 1995).

21. DeLoughry, Thomas. "Purchasing Power: Cost Sharing Efforts Help College Libraries Finance Electronic Acquisitions." *The Chronicle of Higher Education* XLII:A21 (February 9, 1996).

22. "Boston Library Consortium Cooperative Collections Plan," May 1995.

23. Davis, Mary Ellen. "Collaborative Delivery of Electronic Texts Endorsed." *College and Research Library News.* 57:5 (January 1996).

24. Hirshon, Arnold. "Library Strategic Alliances and the Digital Library in the 1990's: the OhioLINK Experience." *Journal of Academic Librarianship.* 21:383 (September 1995).

25. "Resource Sharing: It isn't what it used to be." *OCLC Newsletter* 215:26-28 (May/June 1995).

26. "ARIEL Takes Off Around the World" *RLG News*, Issue 38:12 (Fall 1995).

27. Snyder, Carolyn A. and Beth J. Shapiro. "CIC Resource Sharing Project." *College and Research Library News* 51:22 (January 1990).

28. "NEH Qualifies CRL for $575,000 Challenge Grant." *FOCUS on the Center for Research Libraries* XV:1 (September 1995-February 1996).

29. O'Conner, Phyllis. "Remote Storage Facilities: An Annotated Bibliography." *Serials Review* 20:44 (Summer 1994).

30. Hurt, Charlene. "Building the Foundations of Virginia's Virtual Library." *Information Technology and Libraries.* 14:51 (March 1995).

31. *Ibid.*

32. Cargill, Jennifer. "A Target of Opportunity: Creation of the Louis Network," *Library Hi-Tech* 49-50: 87 (1995).

33. "Michigan Libraries Form Research Triangle." *Library Journal* 117:22 (July 1992).

34. Rogers, Michael. "Florida Libraries Launch Information Network." *Library Journal* 118:22 (June 15, 1993).

35. Weaver-Meyers, Pat and Yem Fong. "Interlibrary Loan and Document Delivery the Debate over Union Lists." *Library Administration and Management* 9:206 (Fall 1995).

36. Boston Library Consortium, Meeting of January 17, 1996 *Board Minutes.*

37. Research Libraries Group. *Press Release: Internet-based WebDOC service for immediate discovery and use of electronic journals.* December 8, 1995.

38. Miller, William. "Electronic Access to Information Will Not Reduce the Costs of Library Materials." *Library Issues.* 15:1 (July 1995).

39. Germain, Charles. "The European Publishing Community and the European Electronic Environment." *Collection Management* 19:132 (1995).

40. Hirschon, *Op. Cit.*, pp. 383-384.

41. "Boston Library Consortium Cooperative Collections Plan," *Op. Cit.*, p. 7.

42. "On Line. How do you find useful resources on the Internet?" *Chronicle of Higher Education* XL:A19 (March 17, 1995).

43. Bowen, William G. "JSTOR and the Economics of Scholarly Communication," a talk given at the Council on Library Resources Conference, Washington, D.C., September 18, 1995, p. 13.

44. Wessling, Julie. "Impact of Holdings on Resource Sharing," *Journal of Library Administration* 21:123 (1995).

45. O' Connor, Phyllis, Susan Wehmeyer, and Susan Weldon. "The Future Using an Integrated Approach: the OhioLINK Experience," *Journal of Library Administration* 21: 117 (1995).

46. Dominguez, Patricia Buck and Luke Swindler. "Cooperative Collection Development in the Research Triangle University Libraries: a Model for the Nation," *College and Research Libraries* 54: 487-489 (November 1993).

47. "Boston Library Consortium Cooperative Collections Plan," *Op. Cit.*, p. 8.

Friends or Predators: Evaluating Academic Periodicals' Price Histories as a Means of Making Subscription Decisions

Anthony W. Ferguson
Kathleen Kehoe

How do you choose your friends? I don't know about you, but I don't include among my list of friends those who seek my downfall. Rather, I look for those who are interested in helping me achieve my goals.

How do you choose what to add to your list of periodicals subscriptions? I would like to suggest that we seek those that help us achieve our research and curricular support goals on the basis of need, quality and price. While establishing a need for a specific title and an analysis of its quality are critical activities, today I would like to focus on the third quality, price, as an important variable. Specifically, I am going to discuss the value of looking at a title's price history as a means of picking one with which you can establish a friendly long-term relationship. I will also discuss ways of combating high prices and the destruction that they bring to our libraries.

Anthony W. Ferguson is Associate University Librarian at Columbia University in New York, NY. Kathleen Kehoe is Reference and Collection Development Librarian at Columbia University in New York, NY.

[Haworth co-indexing entry note]: "Friends or Predators: Evaluating Academic Periodicals' Price Histories as a Means of Making Subscription Decisions." Ferguson, Anthony W., and Kathleen Kehoe. Co-published simultaneously in *Journal of Library Administration* (The Haworth Press, Inc.) Vol. 24, No. 1/2, 1996, pp. 73-85; and: *Emerging Patterns of Collection Development in Expanding Resource Sharing, Electronic Information and Network Environment* (ed: Sul H. Lee) The Haworth Press, Inc., 1996, pp. 73-85. Single or multiple copies of this article are available for a fee from The Haworth Document Delivery Service [1-800-342-9678, 9:00 a.m. - 5:00 p.m. (EST). E-mail address: getinfo@haworth.com].

A year or so ago when thinking about periodicals pricing, I began to personalize the idea of periodicals pricing in terms of some periodicals having friendly pricing practices and others being decidedly unfriendly. Indeed, some periodicals and their publishers seem to take on an aura of the "evil empire." I suggested to a friend of mine who edits a library science periodical that I would like to gather some data on what I felt to be the predatory pricing practices of some publishers, write an article, and submit it to her for publication. After discussing it with her lawyer husband, she told me to hit the road. She observed that some thin-skinned publishers had a habit of litigating such observations and that her husband didn't think she could afford this particular cultural experience.

Undaunted, I decided to collect the data anyway, prepare the paper, and present it at the next opportunity–but to not forewarn the publisher or conference organizer. Luckily, Sul Lee came along and I have this fine opportunity to share my research. The results of this presentation will even be published by one of my favorite publishers. Actually, my presentation is the result of research pursued by myself and Kathleen Kehoe, one of Columbia's finest science librarians. She has agreed to assume the brunt of any future litigation.

For the sake of brevity, I would like to use the terms "friendly periodicals" and "predatory periodicals." In general, I think of friendly periodicals as those which increase in price at a rate even with, or less than, the rate Columbia's library materials budget has increased over the past decade: roughly eight percent per annum. I realize that this level of increase is higher than that experienced by many libraries, but it is the frame of context in which I have been working. By predatory I mean periodicals which have increased at a rate in excess of the rate our budget has increased. I would like to suggest that you make up your own definition of friendly and predator periodicals based upon how your budget has done in recent years. I also use the word predatory because these increases require that other subscriptions be cut or new needs be ignored in favor of maintaining important but repugnantly priced periodicals. Unfortunately, the actual act of cutting other titles or ignoring needs for new materials is carried out by librarians. But the publishers of predatory periodicals set the stage and all but write the script.

Let me now explain the data that will be analyzed. Annually, we request our major periodicals subscription vendor provide us with a five-year pricing history. This report is used to determine which titles are friendly and which are predatory. The most recent report covered the years 1990 to 1995. Using this report, Kathleen and I decided it would be interesting to compare a variety of characteristics for those titles which had increased in price the most with those which had increased the least over this five-year period. We excluded titles we viewed as disposable, e.g., ones that lacked enduring research value. This turned out to be somewhat difficult since some social science magazines lacked the same level of formal credibility possessed by the majority of the science periodicals we analyzed. We further determined to exclude reference works.

We decided to create a group of 75 friendly periodicals and 75 predatory periodicals by drawing a stratified sample. We picked the 15 titles which had increased the most and the 15 that had increased the least (actually most of these decreased in price) in each of five different 1995 pricing levels: $1,000 plus, $500 to $999, $250 to $499, $150 to $249, and $0 to $149. Our choice of price levels was fairly arbitrary. One thousand dollars seemed to be a useful beginning point for the very expensive periodicals. The next step down to $500 cut the distance to $0 in half and the step to $250 was taken for a similar reason. Altogether, we chose our 150 titles from among over 4,000 titles valued in excess of $975,000. This collection of periodicals represents a significant cross-section of Columbia's North American, United Kingdom, and English-language western-European periodicals. Our total periodicals budget for 1995-96 is 2.8 million dollars.

Once we had selected our two groups of 75 periodicals, we gathered a variety of data for each title and group of titles: total and average cost, changes in price, subject, type of publisher, the parent country of the publisher, whether the periodical required page charges from the authors, whether the periodical charged libraries a price different from that charged individuals, and the Institute for Scientific Information impact factor.

Before going through our findings in detail, I would like to summarize for you what we discovered. We determined that predatory periodicals differ from friendly periodicals in a number of significant ways: Because they inflate faster than friendly periodicals (165% versus minus six percent on the average), they cost more, 23% more than friendly titles. Interestingly, if we look beyond the 150 titles analyzed in this study, we find that numerically most of the 4,000 titles on our list are not predatory. More than 65% of all the periodicals on our price history are friendly. This isn't a case where since everyone else is price gouging it is an acceptable norm of behavior. We found that there were predator titles in all subject areas. This isn't just a problem for the sciences. We did determine that foreign periodicals were much more likely to be predatory and that commercially published titles were also more likely to be predators. Finally, we confirmed that predators were also more likely to discriminate to the detriment of libraries in their pricing schemes.

TOTAL AND AVERAGE COST COMPARISONS

While the total cost of the 75 friendly and 75 predatory periodicals did not differ overwhelmingly, the predatory periodicals did cost 23% more: $43,542 for 75 friendly periodicals, $53,697 for 75 predatory periodicals. The average cost of a friendly periodical was $580.56 and $715.96 for a predatory periodical. The highest priced periodical on our list was $8,105.00, and the least costly title was $0.00 for a free title that was sent upon request.

PRICE INCREASES

Since by definition prices for friendly periodicals have inflated the least, it is not surprising that on the average these 75 periodicals decreased in price by minus six percent. Nor is it surprising that the predatory periodicals increased an average of 196%. Of the 4,046 periodicals on our vendor's historical price list, 2,654 or 65.6% grew equal to or less than our budget during the same period of time. On the other hand, 1,392 or 34.4% exceeded the rate of increase experienced by our library materials budget.

We purposely did not attempt to differentiate between inflation caused by a weak dollar, or increases in paper or mailing costs.

Bottom line, irrespective of the reason, when periodicals inflate faster than your library materials budget, you have a problem that is only solved by more money or fewer acquisitions. Good excuses like a devalued dollar do not change reality or help pay serials invoices.

SUBJECT

We classified our periodicals into the three subject groups by which Columbia's libraries are organized: science and engineering, the social sciences, and the humanities. Surprisingly, as shown in Table 1, the percentage of friendly science and engineering periodicals was higher than that for the predatory periodicals. Moreover, the percentage of predatory periodicals for the social sciences and humanities was higher than the figure for science and engineering. While the size of our data is small, it suggests that library problems with high periodicals price increases are not just phenomena for the sciences.

PARENT COUNTRY OF PUBLISHER

We classified our periodicals as foreign or domestic, as shown in Table 2, according to the overall nationality of the publisher. Admittedly, this ignores the difference between US imprints published by a Netherlands publisher or UK imprints published by a US publisher. We wanted to test out the proposition that foreign publishers gouge libraries in the US more than domestic publishers. Unexpect-

TABLE 1. Subject Breakdown of Friendly and Predatory Periodicals

Type/Subject	Friendly No.	Friendly % of Total	Predator No.	Predator % of Total
Science & Engineering	58	55%	48	45%
Social Science	13	38%	21	62%
Humanities	4	40%	6	60%

TABLE 2. National Origin of Friendly and Predatory Periodicals Publishers

Type/Publisher	Friendly No.	Friendly % of Total	Predator No.	Predator % of Total
Domestic	22	33%	45	67%
Foreign	53	64%	30	36%

edly, however, we found that there were more than twice as many foreign publishers represented in the friendly group of periodicals as there were among the predatory periodicals. What this means is that, even with dollar devaluation as a potential scapegoat, domestic publishers in our study were actually worse than foreign publishers in the production of predatory periodicals.

Of the 53 friendly foreign periodicals, 12 were published by a UK-based publisher, 12 by a Netherlands publisher, and the other 20 in nine other countries. Thirteen of the predatory titles were published by a UK publisher, 14 by a Netherlands publisher, and the other three titles were published in two other countries.

PUBLISHER TYPE

We were also interested in determining whether predatory publishers were more likely to be commercial publishers than other types of publishers. Consequently, we classified the publishers of our periodicals, see Table 3, as societies or associations, commercial, or commercial in behalf of a society or association. In this case the stereotype proved to be true. While it is correct that society/association publishers are one-third less likely to produce predatory periodicals (Society/association publishers accounted for 32 friendly titles and only 22 predator titles), when you add the number of titles published by commercial publishers for societies and associations to the ones published directly by commercial publishers, fifty-five percent of the predatory titles are published by commercial publishers. While a 10% difference is not an overwhelming one, it is still the case that commercial publishers increase their prices faster than

TABLE 3. Type of Friendly and Predatory Publishers

Type/Publisher	Friendly No.	Friendly % of Total	Predator No.	Predator % of Total
Society/Association	32	59%	22	41%
Commercial	37	49%	39	51%
Commercial for Soc./Assn.	6	30%	14	70%
Combined Commercial	43	45%	53	55%

others. We definitely have a problem. Librarians and scholars see periodicals as mediums of information dissemination. Some publishers see them as profitable investments. Robert Maxwell is quoted as characterizing his journal operation as "A cash generator twice over."[1] When we consider starting subscriptions, we need to remember that we are starting something that, for reasons not related to scholarship, may grow faster in price than we will have the means to keep up with the payments. In no other part of our life would we consider buying something, like a house or car, the payment price of which was likely to increase from 10% to 20% faster than our income. Somehow, we have allowed this phenomenon to become an accepted part of our library culture.

DISCRIMINATORY PRICING

We were interested in finding out if friendly titles were any different from predatory titles in terms of discriminatory prices charged to libraries. That is, do they charge libraries differently than individuals? As shown in Table 4, predatory periodicals were much more likely to discriminate than were friendly periodicals, according to whether the subscriber was a library or not. When looking for this information in each of the titles analyzed, our fears about some publishers were strengthened by the following statement located in the subscription information section: "[X] will pay a reward of up to $1,000 for actionable evidence of illegal copying or faxing."

TABLE 4. Discriminatory Pricing Practices of Friendly and Predatory Periodicals Publishers

Type/Publisher	Friendly No.	Friendly % of Total	Predator No.	Predator % of Total
Doesn't Discriminate	40	62%	25	38%
Discriminates	35	41%	50	59%

While not a case of discriminatory pricing, this 10-page-per-issue periodical had increased in price by 449% over the course of the last five years.

PAGE CHARGES

We thought we would like to examine the issue of page charges. Hypothetically, publishers who charge authors something to cover the cost of publication do so to keep the cost of their periodicals down and those who forego this kind of revenue have to make up for the loss by charging their subscribers. Actually, among the 75 friendly and 75 predator periodicals, very few utilized page charges: four friendly, five predator.

ICE IMPACT FACTOR

We also wanted to be able to qualitatively compare the quality of our friendly and predatory periodicals. Hopefully, in the spirit of "you get what you pay for," the quality of the periodicals which were able to raise their prices faster than others would prove to be better periodicals. We decided to try to employ the Institute for Scientific Information's Impact Factor as the means of comparing quality. The definition of an Impact Factor is "the average number of times articles published in a specific periodical in the two previous years were cited in a particular year."[2] The higher the impact factor the better. Unfortunately, as shown in Table 5, only 17 friendly periodicals and 19 predator periodicals had Impact Factors. While this number is too low to say anything definitive a much higher percentage of the predator titles had a higher than a "1" ranking than the friendly titles. This would seem to support the contention that more valuable periodicals can and do charge more.

CONCLUSIONS

So there are predators out there. What else is new? What can we do about it? Overall, I would like to suggest that we acknowledge that we are in an adversarial position with some titles and their publishers, and deal with it. If we don't, we will continue to be victims.

Basically, I think the following five steps should be taken to curtail the power that predatory journals have had upon us in the past. We need to:

1. *Look backward before going forward.* Whenever possible, we need to examine at least five years of price data before initiating a subscription. The data ably demonstrates that there are predatory titles which, if allowed to go unchecked, will push us into killing off some titles or areas of collecting in order to continue feeding these carnivores.

Obviously, if we need a new periodical for which there is not a pricing history, this is impossible. However, we can spend the extra energy to monitor these new titles over the succeeding years to decide as soon as possible if we can afford them. There is a significant likelihood that the initial price may increase at predatory levels.

If we do have the data, however, we should subscribe only when

TABLE 5. ICE Ratings for Friendly and Predatory Periodicals

Type/ ICE Level	Friendly No.	Friendly % of Total	Predator No.	Predator % of Total
Higher than 1	8	40%	12	60%
Lower than 1	9	56%	7	44%

we feel that we can afford to buy a title that will continue to inflate at the past rate of increase. Even if it is a foreign title with currency problems, our understanding the problem won't help pay the bills.

2. *Target predators, not publishers.* For existing subscriptions, we need to target titles, for use studies and faculty evaluation, that inflate faster than our budget increases. We need to put book mark surveys in new issues that say "This title has increased X% over the past year. Do you think we should continue to subscribe? Cancel? Continue to monitor?" We need to let our users check off what they think and then take the appropriate action. This is better than targeting specific publishers, although there may be a correlation between predatory periodicals and some publishers.

3. *Involve the faculty.* We need to send our faculty lists of the worst offenders since they may not read these titles themselves. We should also give them document delivery information for each title, e.g., whether a table of contents service you might have provides coverage and the copyright charge levied for each article. We need to ask them if they think these periodicals are justified in raising prices at the rates shown by our five-year price history data and if they would accept document delivery as a substitute for a subscription. A recent study suggests that high prices are the result of too little competition between journals, and readers being insulated from pricing information.[3]

4. *Notify editors and publishers.* We should send the editors and publishers of the worst offenders letters indicating that we are targeting their titles for faculty evaluation and use studies. We should also send the editors and publishers of high quality friendly periodicals thank you notes for keeping their prices down.

5. *Cancel loudly.* After we have gathered our user surveys and faculty input, we need to go back to the faculty and seek their support for the cancellation of titles whose price history and user and faculty evaluation suggest that these are not friends of our libraries. When we do cancel a title, we should write its editor and publisher telling them why their title was canceled. Be sure to send copies of letters to the chair of the relevant department since the publisher, and or editor, will probably appeal to members of the department for amnesty for their title.

Now of course there will be many in this audience who will say, if large numbers of libraries cancel a title, the publisher will simply retaliate by further raising the price of that periodical or another periodical in their family of titles to the detriment of other subscribers. I agree. This seems to have happened in the past, so it will probably happen in the future. However, if enough of the remaining subscribers practice the five rules mentioned above, publishers will soon decide they have to find new ways of working with their library subscribers.

Is it possible that publishers and libraries can accommodate each other's needs? I think it is possible, but it will require a departure from past practices. I would like to suggest that publishers and libraries sit down together and sign contractual agreements in which rate increases acceptable to both parties are established. (Yes, Virginia, there is a Santa Claus.) If we don't do something different, we will continue down a path to mutual destruction. Let me share with you what I would call Price Models A and B. They are both grounded in reality, but they are, of course, exaggerations of what is really the case. They describe how two very different pricing schemes designed to achieve the same rate of gross revenue increase can end in either destruction or managed survival.

Both models describe a situation in which a publisher in 1995 produced 25 titles and sold 1,000 subscriptions, each priced at $20. Libraries subscribing to all 25 titles in 1995 would each pay a total of $500. However, in the ensuing years the pricing schemes diverge and the consequences also become quite different.

Model A (Table 6) could be labeled as the "mutual suicide" model. It ultimately destroys both publishers and libraries. In this model, even though the publisher annually raises the price by 20%, higher prices reduce sales by six percent and gross revenues are negatively impacted. If continued, by the year 2035 the unit cost will increase from $20 to $29,395 per year and the number of copies printed will have fallen from 1,000 to 195. Perhaps there are other industries where the business plan dictates a goal of decreased production, but this seems insane to me. While the figures in this model may be remote from reality, they reflect what is really taking place. Moreover, librarians faced with these kinds of price increases are seeking alternative modes of information delivery and many

TABLE 6. Model A: Mutual Suicide, Annual 6% Decrease in Sales and 20% Increase in Price

Year	No. Titles published	Unit price: 20% annual increase	Units sold: 6% annual decrease	Publisher gross revenue ($000)	Percent change in gross revenue	Library annual subscription cost
1995	25	$20	1,000	$500	xxxx	$500
1996	25	$24	960	$576	15%	$600
1997	25	$29	922	$665	15%	$720
1998	25	$35	885	$764	15%	$864
1999	25	$41	849	$881	15%	$1,037
2000	25	$50	815	$1,014	15%	$1,244
2001	25	$60	783	$1,169	15%	$1,493
2002	25	$72	751	$1,346	15%	$1,792
2003	25	$86	721	$1,550	15%	$2,150
2004	25	$103	693	$1,787	15%	$2,580
2035	25	$29,395	195	$143,572	15%	$734,886

TABLE 7. Model B: Steady State License, Annual 6% Increase in Sales and 8% Increase in Price

Year	No. Titles published	Unit price: 8.5% annual increase	Units sold: 6% annual increase	Publisher gross revenue ($000)	Percent change in gross revenue	Library annual subscription cost
1995	25	$20	1,000	$500	xxxx	$500
1996	25	$22	1,060	$575	15%	$543
1997	25	$24	1,124	$661	15%	$589
1998	25	$26	1,191	$761	15%	$639
1999	25	$28	1,262	$875	15%	$693
2000	25	$30	1,338	$1,006	15%	$752
2001	25	$33	1,419	$1,157	15%	$816
2002	25	$35	1,504	$1,331	15%	$885
2003	25	$38	1,594	$1,531	15%	$960
2004	25	$42	1,689	$1,760	15%	$1,042
2035	25	$523	10,286	$134,398	15%	$13,067

want to take copyright away from publishers as a means of reducing their power.

Model B, as illustrated by Table 7, suggests that if libraries were willing to agree upon an increase as high as 8.5% per annum and publishers were willing to live within that amount of increased revenue, libraries would not be taxed to distraction and publishers could focus on expanding their subscriber base. In this model, the motivation to cancel periodicals is much reduced. The need for new journals would produce a parallel need to cancel old subscriptions, but the cyclical slash and burn mentality of canceling hundreds of thousands of dollars' worth of subscriptions by major research libraries will be considerably lessened.

Two alternative courses of action have been presented here. The first assumes that there will be predatory periodicals, and that if libraries follow a five-step formula, the predators will become the prey. The second suggests that publishers and libraries can help each other by each giving up some of their freedom of action. I think it is time to try something different. I welcome calls from major publishers interested in negotiating price licenses.

NOTES

1. Michael A. Stoller, Robert Christopherson and Michael Miranda, "The Economics of Professional Journal Pricing," *College and Research Libraries* 57 (January 1996):15.

2. *Journal Citation Reports on CD-ROM, Quick Reference Guide.* (Philadelphia: Institute for Scientific Information, Inc., 1995): 12.

3. Stoller, 13-14.

Collecting, Sharing, and Networking: The Role and Responsibilities of a National Library

William J. Sittig

PART I

National libraries are usually the most important and largest libraries in their countries, regardless of the size or wealth of these countries. They exercise considerable influence not only within their respective nations' boundaries but also beyond—in the larger international community of libraries and scholarship. Although each national library has its own core functions and priorities, most are responsible for collecting, organizing, and preserving their nations' imprints and sharing the contents of their collections, either directly or indirectly, with their governmental officials and their citizenry. As grand and important as they are, however, national libraries are affected and influenced by the same forces that affect and influence other libraries—the principal ones being economic and technological. In this paper I will describe how economic and technological forces are changing the collection and dissemination policies and practices of several national libraries, and then I will focus particularly on the Library of Congress.

The typical national library's collection is based principally on the national imprint, with foreign publications and documents assuming a subsidiary or supporting role. Some libraries, of course, continue to collect extensively the publications of their former colonies, as is the case of the Dutch for Indonesian materials. The national imprint, which is acquired usually through the instrument of legal deposit, can be confined to books and serials but may include other formats such as maps, prints, and sound recordings, as well as manuscripts, and other original documents significant to the national heritage. The collection policies and goals of the national libraries of two disparate countries are illustrative:

> The focus of the National Library [of Canada] is directed in particular to the custody and promotion of our heritage as it is reflected in publication. Gathering, preserving, and making accessible Canadiana, defined as works published in Canada, works by Canadians published abroad, and foreign publications bearing on Canadian subjects, the National Library endeavors to ensure that the published sources needed to understand and interpret Canada as a nation and as a culture are readily available not only to today's scholars and researchers, but to those who succeed us in generations to come.[1]

As of today, the legal deposit in Canada provides for two copies of monographs, serials, music, sound recordings, microforms, educational kits, audio and video tapes, and CD-ROMs.

The collecting policy of the National Library of Poland, the Biblioteka Narodowa, decreed in August 1992 as part of the Statute of the National Library, is as follows:

> The Library shall acquire, process, store and make available the collections, that is to say: prints [printed works], manuscripts, iconographic materials, maps, music, audiovisual, electronic—both original and reproduced—comprising:
>
> 1. written documents and monuments of Polish culture,
> 2. the entirety of book production of the Republic of Poland,
> 3. all Polish or Poland-related publications published abroad,
> 4. foreign literature indispensable for the development of Polish science and culture in the field of social sciences and

humanities, with special relation to library and information science, in accordance with the specialization of research libraries in the country, [and]
5. iconographic, cartographic, music, electronic documents which were produced in Poland or are Poland-related, and foreign prints.[2]

These two libraries are typical in that they have long striven for comprehensive collections of the national output as well as for substantial collections of foreign materials, especially in the areas of science and technology and politics and law, to support domestic research and governmental operations. They are also typical in that they have found that governmental and, where it exists, private financial support has not been sufficient to acquire, provide bibliographic control of, and preserve such collections. Limited available resources and high costs have long been the situation in the less developed countries, but they are now a reality for a growing number of national libraries in the "rich" nations. As a result, they have had to make difficult choices in scaling back their collecting practices and relating in new ways to the research and public libraries in their respective countries.

As aptly explained by Dr. Marianne Scott, National Librarian of Canada, in a presentation at McGill University in November 1994:

> the economic atmosphere changed during the 1980s and budgets have tightened even more sharply during the 1990s. When we conducted a major review of the National Library's program objectives in 1986, we knew we had to contend with increasing costs, decreasing finances, repairs and modifications to an aging building . . . and exciting but costly new directions in technological development. It was time to rethink priorities.[3]

As a result of this rethinking, the National Library of Canada reaffirmed its commitment to maintaining and serving its strong collection of Canadiana but scaled back its practice of collecting and maintaining non-Canadian materials. Foreign serial collecting was reduced significantly, and parts of existing serial collections actually were distributed to other libraries across the country. The focus of their non-Canadiana collecting now is limited to support of Canadian music, literature, reference, and a few other subject areas.[4] Commitments to a complete union catalog of Canadiana in machine-readable format and a strong interlibrary lending program are important components of this new direction. Dr. Scott noted that "Networking and resource sharing simply [became] a higher priority."[5]

Even Japan, a country which until recently was not affected by declining economic resources, has moved toward a more networked environment. A recent publication of the National Diet Library (NDL) states:

> In view of the steady and remarkable development of the public and university libraries witnessed over recent years, the NDL has gradually been shifting its emphasis toward highlighting its basic position as the nation's library of last resort, having rationalized the service points for those libraries while at the same time encouraging the prefectural and other major public libraries to commit themselves further as the node of each of the emerging regional networks.[6]

The National Library of Australia has taken, perhaps, the most dramatic steps to alter its collecting policies in accord with fiscal realities. When its predecessor, the Commonwealth Parliamentary Library, was founded in the first decade of this century, its objective, in the words of the Joint Parliamentary Library Committee, was the establishment of "in the Federal Capital, a great public Library on the lines of the world-famed Library of Congress at Washington; such a Library, indeed, as shall be worthy of the Australian nation; the home of the literature, not of a State, or of a period, but of the world, and of all time."[7] Although the Library was never able to attain these lofty goals, it has been able to accumulate the world's largest collections of materials relating to Australia and respectable holdings of foreign materials. In the late 1980s, however, a constellation of economic factors—namely, the continuing decline of the Australian dollar in relation to other currencies; government policies which placed a cost on materials previously donated by government institutions; and similar costs placed by foreign governments on documents and other materials previously donated, deposited, or exchanged free of charge—necessitated the issuance of a new collection development policy of more constricted ambition.

The National Library will still collect Australian imprints (although it will reduce its intake of state and local publications and other materials not considered of *national* significance) and will severely reduce its foreign collections to include only materials from areas of most immediate significance to Australian political and economic interests. Southeast Asia and Pacific Island materials now are taking a higher priority than are materials from Europe, the Americas, and other parts of the world. The National Library announced its new policy at the Australian Libraries Summit in 1988 and received a strong endorsement for what is formally called "a distributed national collection." The Library is achieving this coordinated objective by encouraging wide participation in completing the Australian Conspectus and assuming responsibility for creating and distributing the online National Bibliographic Database.

The dissemination of bibliographic information by electronic means displaying not only the library's own holdings but, in many cases, the holdings of other libraries of the country, is an increasingly common and important use of the advanced technologies by national libraries. What is new and exciting is the opportunity offered by electronic technology to provide access not only to bibliographic data and other information, such as the library's services and products, but also to the contents of the collections themselves. This can be seen as an extension of national libraries' responsibilities to share the national patrimony, which hitherto has been limited to on-site use and, for some materials, by inter-library lending.

Several widely publicized efforts are worth mentioning briefly. One of the more ambitious is the British Library's "Initiative for Access," a program of twenty development projects suggested by its 1993 *Strategic Objectives* for the year 2000. In this plan, the Library undertook "to investigate the means of providing maximum access to the existing collections, which include books, journals, patents, photographs, manuscripts, stamps and sound recordings, for on-site and remote users through the exploitation of digital and networking technologies."[8] Among the projects are "Electronic *Beowulf*," the digitization of the complete text of the original manuscript by high resolution cameras under white light, ultraviolet light, and with a fiber-optic pad; the digitization of some heavily used microfilm sets, such as the Burney Collection of eighteenth-century newspapers; the "Electronic Photo Viewing System," which will enable picture researchers to access some major photograph collections, such as the Indian miniatures and portraits of Victorian spiritualists; and the digitization of some of the major treasures of written and printed materials displayed in the Library's Bloomsbury galleries.

Some other examples include the digitization by the Royal Library of the Netherlands of manuscripts, rare books, and other specimens from the exhibition "A Hundred Highlights"; the National Library of Canada's providing on its World Wide Web server an electronic exhibit on the Canadian composer Sir Ernest MacMillan; and the joint project of the Vatican Library and IBM to digitize selected images from that Library's rich collections. The National Library of New Zealand announced in its 1994 report *Strategic Directions* that "the Library reached a historic agreement with the National Library of Australia to develop a joint computer system — the National Document and Information Service" which will enable users "to access the Library's catalogues, view full-text copies of items as well as images of pictures, maps and photographs, and request copies of items of interest."[9]

Finally, it is worth noting that national libraries are playing a prominent role in the Electronic Libraries project endorsed by the leaders of the Group of Seven (G7) industrialized nations (United States, Canada, France, United Kingdom, Italy, Germany, and Japan) at their Information Society Summit held in Brussels, February 1995. This project, one of eleven intended to demonstrate the potential of the Information Society and stimulate its deployment, has as its goal "to constitute from existing digitisation programs a large distributed virtual collection of the knowledge of mankind, available to the public via networks. This includes a clear perspective towards the establishment of the global electronic library network which interconnects local electronic libraries."[10]

As a word of caution, Federico Mayor, Director General of UNESCO, speaking at the time of the conference, stressed:

> [I]t is crucial in this context that the global information infrastructure should be more than just a system of information superhighways. The most urgent and painful education needs are among population groups which may reside in some of the 600,000 villages throughout the world that are still without electricity. . . . The global information system must cater to the whole of the world community and not simply to those who have the means to frequent its main thoroughfares.[11]

Heeding Director General Mayor's words and representing the best instincts of national librarians, the National Librarian of Canada, Dr. Scott, speaking in Victoria, British Columbia, at the international forum "Networking the Pacific," stated:

> In a world of scarce resources and disparities of wealth, the spirit of open access to information at the heart of librarianship functions as a moral imperative to assist libraries in countries whose technical, financial and information resources are less developed. Herein are the real benefits of networking at the international level: the ability to facilitate and coordinate information flows to all countries, including the developing countries, and to encourage an understanding of the diversity of the global cultural heritage.[12]

PART II

The United States has two officially designated national libraries and one de facto national library. The Department of Agriculture's library, which was established in 1862 when President Lincoln signed the Organic Act, was designated a national library over a century later with the mission "to acquire and to diffuse among the people of the United States useful information on subjects connected with agriculture and rural development, in the most general and comprehensive sense of those terms."[13] Evolving from the library in the Office of the Surgeon General in the Medical Department of the Army, the National Library of Medicine officially came into being when a bill submitted by Senators Lister Hill and John F. Kennedy "to promote the progress of medicine and to advance the national health and welfare by creating a National Library of Medicine"[14] was signed into law on August 3, 1956. This act empowered the Library to "acquire and preserve books, periodicals, prints, films, recordings and other library materials pertinent to medicine"[15] in order to fulfill its mandate to serve health professionals.

Although initially created as a legislative library only, it would be difficult to deny that the Library of Congress is the national library of the United States. As so eloquently described and documented by Dr. John Y. Cole in his many writings on the subject,[16] the pivotal moment when LC became the de facto national library was the centralization of all U.S. copyright deposit and registration activities at the Library by the Copyright Act of 1870, so persistently and successfully advocated by Librarian Ainsworth Rand Spofford. When the Library occupied its magnificent new building in 1897 and had accumulated the largest collection in the United States, primarily due to the copyright receipts, it was universally acknowledged that the Library of Congress was the national library. Congress, too, has acknowledged on many occasions the larger role of "its library," usually with pride. Statements before the House of Representatives on January 18, 1961, by two Congressmen of different political parties are illustrative: Omar Burleson, a Texas Democrat who had served as chair and vice chair of the Joint Committee on the Library, stated that the Library of Congress "is, in effect, the national library of the United States. That it is in the legislative branch is entirely fitting, for, historically, its first duty is to serve the Nation through the Congress."[17] Speaking later, Fred Schwengel, Republican from Iowa, remarked, "The Congress created the Library of Congress and saw it through its tragedies and its triumphs until today it is, in fact, the national library of the United States, one of the great cultural institutions of the world."[18]

In the late 1960s, when the National Advisory Commission on Libraries was studying the status of libraries in the United States, it pronounced that LC, in addition to its services to Congress, performs more typical national library functions than any other national library. These functions, which, for the most part, are still being performed, are:

1. Collecting comprehensively, not only the national heritage but also materials from every country of the world;
2. Benefitting from copyright, legal deposits, and intergovernmental exchanges;
3. Receiving gifts to the nation of personal papers, rare books, and trust funds;
4. Administering a worldwide acquisitions program;
5. Devising and maintaining classification and subject-heading systems that serve as national standards;
6. Serving as the national center for cataloging;
7. Administering a national distribution service of catalog cards and bibliographic data on magnetic tape;
8. Publishing the national bibliography;
9. Maintaining other union catalogs;
10. Providing reference services, on site and by mail, and operating such "switchboards" as the National Referral Service;
11. Participating in interlibrary loan and photocopying services;
12. Maintaining an active bibliographic and publications program;
13. Administering a national program for the blind and physically handicapped;
14. Presenting concerts, literary programs, and exhibitions to enrich the cultural life of the nation;
15. Experimenting and conducting research in library technology;
16. Playing a leading role in developing and implementing techniques and procedures for the preservation of library materials; and
17. Engaging in national and international cooperative programs.[19]

The main basis for its acknowledged position as the national library is its vast and increasing collections of materials in every recorded form, from books and manuscripts to tapes of television programs and digital geographic and cartographic data, in all written languages and from every country of the world. Indeed, if it were not for the collections, most of the aforementioned functions and services would not be possible.

The Library's collection policies are guided by the Canons of Selection, first articulated by Librarian Archibald MacLeish in

1940, and espoused, as modified and updated, by all subsequent Librarians of Congress. The Canons stipulate in priority order that the Library should possess in some useful form (1) all bibliothecal materials necessary to the Congress and to the officers of the government of the United States in the performance of their duties; (2) all books and other materials which express and record the life and achievements of the people of the United States; and (3) the material parts of the records of other societies, past and present, and full and representative collections of the written records of those societies and people whose experience is of most immediate concern to the people of the United States.[20]

The present Librarian of Congress, Dr. James H. Billington, has consistently endorsed these precepts. He has recently announced that the Library's mission is "to make its resources available and useful to the Congress and the American people and to sustain and preserve a universal collection of knowledge and creativity for the future generations." A high priority is the acquisition, preservation and sustenance of a comprehensive record of American history and creativity and a universal (with the exception of technical agriculture and clinical medicine) collection of human knowledge. He justified the continuation of broad and inclusive collections because:

- far more knowledge is being generated in more ways, more places and more formats than in the past;
- the knowledge needs of Congress and government are becoming more complex than ever before as we enter the information age in a competitive international environment where Americans will increasingly have to rely on better use of knowledge to succeed; and
- the access needs of Congress, the U.S. government, and the thinking and creative public cannot be made hostage to the collection and deaccession policies and priorities of other less comprehensive and less nationally accountable institutions.[21]

Given the Library of Congress's commitment to comprehensive and universal collections, how is it coping with the economic realities affecting other national libraries? Let there be no doubt, at present and for the foreseeable future, the level of funding available from the U.S. government will not be growing. Regardless of who wins the upcoming presidential election or which political party controls Congress, the mood is one of governmental retrenchment and reduced appropriations. Congress traditionally has been generous to the Library of Congress, but it would be reckless to think that the agency will be spared the budget axe. Recent appropriations for acquisitions reflected a 4.1% increase for fiscal year 1995 and a 0% increase for fiscal year 1996. Although this was an increase in dollar amount appropriations, it was not enough to keep up with price level increases of library materials. The price increases, as calculated by the Library of Congress Order Division, were 5.7% for fiscal year 1995 and 4.2% for fiscal year 1996. This leaves us in the position of trying to walk up the down escalator. Our feet are moving forward, but we aren't gaining ground. How has the Library accommodated to a static appropriated base while striving to develop and sustain comprehensive collections?

First, the Library is cooperating with the other two U.S. national libraries to reduce unnecessary redundancies in collecting practices. Monographs and serials on medical and agricultural subjects which are clearly in scope for NLM and NAL and clearly out of scope for LC are being transferred to the appropriate institution, and collecting in these areas has been discontinued. There will, of course, always be some overlap of materials held by the three institutions because of the immediate service needs of their respective users, but approximately 21,000 volumes have been deaccessioned from the Library's collections.

Second, LC is actively participating in the ARL Foreign Acquisitions projects in the anticipation that, through cooperative arrangements, we may be able to rely more on other repositories, both foreign and domestic, to collect and share lesser-used materials. It is too early to know to what extent LC will be able to forgo collecting certain titles, but we remain optimistic that there will be tangible results of long-term savings.

Third, like every other institution represented here, LC has had to reduce its serial holdings. Our first reduction was achieved by removing from our materials budget subscriptions to office and personal copies of newspapers and journals which were not added to the research collections. Then, we reviewed and cancelled subscriptions to multiple copies of serials assigned to many different reading rooms, compelling increased sharing of resources among reference divisions. We also cancelled hard copy subscriptions to titles available through online services, such as OCLC FirstSearch, although we retain one inkprint copy of each title for archival purposes. In addition, we cancelled over $40,000 worth of subscriptions to foreign newspapers, most of which were unique copies. Most significantly, in order to reduce future demands on the serial budget, for the past two years we have placed subscriptions for only the highest priority new serial titles. For several months now there has been a moratorium on ordering any new priced subscriptions. Our Collections Policy Committee will determine how long this moratorium will last and what other measures will be taken to reduce serial costs.

Fourth and last, increased efforts are being made to obtain private funding for the acquisition of special collections and rarities. The Madison Council, the Library's private sector advisory and support group, has established an Acquisitions Committee to obtain funding for special purchases, and senior staff and curators are working with other private individuals and corporations to support this activity. Special collections, especially the creative output of prominent Americans, have long been an essential part of the national collections, but the costs for their acquisition, processing, and preservation have been increasing at rates higher than our appropriations can accommodate.

Like other national libraries, the Library of Congress is taking advantage of the new electronic technologies to fulfill its historical role of disseminating its collections as broadly as possible and to assume a leadership role in the United States and abroad in developing a national and even global digital library. These have been important goals of Dr. Billington since he assumed his position as Librarian of Congress. In an interview for *The Washington Post* in 1994, Dr. Billington said that eventually he hoped that the Library's full collection will be available electronically. "We have a responsibility to share more information with more people," he said.[22] "This is our way of giving back to the American people the collections they have built with their tax support," stated Suzanne Thorin, chair of the Library's Digital Library Coordinating Committee, in another forum.[23]

The Library of Congress was instrumental, in partnership with the Commission on Preservation and Access, in establishing the National Digital Library Federation. Comprising fourteen other research libraries and archives, the Federation has a goal of increased access to research collections conforming to the general theme of U.S. heritage and culture. The participants agreed to "establish a collaborative management structure, develop a coordinated approach to fund-raising and formulate selection guidelines."[24]

A principal contribution of the Library to the national digitization effort is the conversion of some of its primary materials and historical collections to digital form for widespread distribution. Beginning in 1990 with the prototype American Memory program, LC has digitized and made available on the World Wide Web over fifteen collections, including selected Civil War photographs from the Matthew Brady and other collections, 1861-65; early films of San Francisco before and after the earthquake and fire, 1897-1907; life histories from the WPA Folklore Project, 1936-39; and films of President William McKinley and the Pan-American Exposition, 1901. A significant recent addition is the collection of more than 25,000 vintage photographs from the collection of the Detroit Publishing Company, one of the largest American publishers of photographic views and postcards, dating from 1880 to 1920.

The Library's goal is to convert five million items to digital form by the year 2000. Robert Zich, Director of Electronic Programs, in the National Digital Library program, speculated recently[25] that, with improving technology at lower costs and an expected increase in the acquisition of materials in digitized form through copyright deposit and other means, perhaps half of the Library's 220 million-item collection will be digital by the year 2030. This forecast is highly speculative, but there can be little doubt that LC's and other libraries' collections will have a radically different character early in the next century.

Other important contributions that the Library is making to the national digital effort, in collaboration with other libraries and the private sector, include resolving copyright issues by developing an electronic copyright management system and pilot projects that experiment with blanket licenses and royalty payments for non-profit uses; determining appropriate levels and types of access for digital materials; and improving electronic services to Congress and the Library's other users.[26]

CONCLUSION

As befits a proper conclusion, I would like to tie together the various strands of this presentation to confidently predict that the opportunities offered to national and other libraries by the new electronic technologies will successfully resolve the problems caused by shrinking financial resources. This, however, may not be the case. For instance, we know that the costs of developing, acquiring, and using electronic systems will not be low. Efficiencies to be gained by their utilization, such as the greater accessibility to information that does not have to be "owned" and the resultant requirement for less space to house printed materials, may be achieved, only to be offset by the costs of providing intellectual access to greater amounts of unsorted information, the preservation of electronic information stored in ways that soon become obsolete, and meeting heavier user demands for access to an increasing array of information more rapidly.

There may, however, be some cause for optimism. In the case of LC, the Congress has generously supported the American Memory project and its successor programs as a means to share more widely with the American people unique and historically important resources. These efforts have been favorably received across the country. By being better able to fulfill one of the Library's primary national responsibilities, support for basic services, such as collecting and processing library materials, may be sustained. There is hope that the electronic information and network environment will permit, through expanded resource sharing, the continuation of the development of national collections for the benefit of all of our constituencies.

NOTES

1. National Library of Canada. *Orientations: a Planning Framework for the 1990s* (Ottawa, 1989), p. 4.

2. An English translation of the Statute of the National Library, issued as Decree no. 21, effective Aug. 6, 1992, was kindly furnished by Hanna Zielinska,

Head, Acquisition and Processing Division, and Ewa Krysiak, Head, Union Catalogs and Electronic Information Center, of the National Library of Poland.

3. Marianne Scott, "The National Library of Canada: Future Challenges" (presentation to library students at McGill University, Nov. 11, 1994, photocopy), 5.

4. *Ibid.*, 6.

5. *Ibid.*, 6.

6. Kokuritsu Kokkai Toshokan, *National Diet Library* (Tokyo, 1992), pp. 23-24.

7. National Library of Australia, *Collection Development Policy* (Melbourne, 1990), p. 1.

8. British Library, "Initiatives for Access," in Portico, the British Library's Online Information Server (London, 1993).

9. National Library of New Zealand, *Strategic Directions* (Wellington, 1994), p. 9.

10. "The Information Society," *Online & CDROM Review* 19 (1995): 97-98.

11. *Ibid.*, pp. 95, 96.

12. Marianne Scott, "The Role of the National Library in International Networking" (paper presented at "Networking the Pacific," an international forum, Victoria, B.C., May 1995), 3.

13. *Revised Statutes* sec. 520, as amended by U.S. Public Law 92-419 sec. 603(a), in *U.S. Statutes at Large* 86 (1973): 675.

14. *Congressional Record*, 84th Cong., 2d sess., 1956, 102, pt. 4: 4532.

15. *U.S. Statutes at Large* 70 (1957): 960.

16. See especially his "Of Copyright, Men & a National Library," *Quarterly Journal of the Library of Congress* 28 (1971): 114-36, and "For Congress & the Nation: the Dual Nature of the Library of Congress," *Quarterly Journal of the Library of Congress* 32 (1975): 118-38.

17. *Congressional Record*, 87th Cong., 1st sess., 1961, 107, pt. 1: 978.

18. *Annual Report of the Librarian of Congress for the Fiscal Year Ending June 30, 1962* (Washington: USGPO, 1963), p. 95.

19. "The Library of Congress as the National Library: Potentialities for Service," chap. 10 in *Libraries at Large*, ed. Douglas M. Knight and E. Shipley Nourse (New York: R. R. Bowker, 1969), pp. 444-45.

20. *Annual Report of the Librarian of Congress for the Fiscal Year Ended June 30, 1940* (Washington: USGPO, 1941), pp. 24-26.

21. James H. Billington, "The Mission and Strategic Priorities of the Library of Congress" (U.S. Library of Congress, Washington, D.C., 1995, photocopy), pp. 1-2.

22. Elizabeth Corcoran, "Bit by Bit, an On-Line Collection," *Washington Post*, 10 October 1994, sec. A, p. 8.

23. Gail Fineberg, "Staff to Hear Digital Library Details," *Gazette* (Library of Congress) 7 April 1995, 1.

24. "Library of Congress Signs National Digital Library Federation Agreement," *Library of Congress News*, PR95-86, May 24, 1995.

25. Robert Zich, "The Future of Libraries," *Wired* 3 (December 1995): 68.

26. See "Strategic Directions Toward a Digital Library Coalition; a Working Paper" (Library of Congress, 11 October 1994, photocopy).

Emerging Patterns of Partnership in Collection Development: A Subscription Vendor's Perspective

Kit Kennedy

"Trust me." "Trust me."

Depending upon your perspective, your experience with vendors, these words, "Trust me," might be words to scare, words to give wide berth. Yet, these words are no more, no less words of petition, of invitation. In short, words asking whether partnership is, if not inevitable, at least a possibility.

I am a vendor–have been a vendor for quite some time, long enough to begin marking the time by decades. I am no visionary, no prophet, no strategist, no artist–alas, the list continues–no inspired and inspiring administrator, no absolute risk-taker, no revolutionary, no scholar, no philosopher. I observe. I listen. I am a teller of stories, a repeater of tales. I am a vendor. (References to vendor in this paper refer to "subscription agents" in their fullest manifestations.)

What story is to shared, what tale spun? What observations offered? I suggest we begin with a beginning, surf to a middle, and in pure Internet fashion wonder where we are, how we got here, who is with us, who is not with us and why, and how we can get out

---

Kit Kennedy is Director, Academic Sales for Readmore Academic Services in San Francisco, CA.

[Haworth co-indexing entry note]: "Emerging Patterns of Partnership in Collection Development: A Subscription Vendor's Perspective." Kennedy, Kit. Co-published simultaneously in *Journal of Library Administration* (The Haworth Press, Inc.) Vol. 24, No. 1/2, 1996, pp. 103-111; and: *Emerging Patterns of Collection Development in Expanding Resource Sharing, Electronic Information and Network Environment* (ed: Sul H. Lee) The Haworth Press, Inc., 1996, pp. 103-111. Single or multiple copies of this article are available for a fee from The Haworth Document Delivery Service [1-800-342-9678, 9:00 a.m. - 5:00 p.m. (EST). E-mail address: getinfo@haworth.com].

of it, how we get back home. These questions bring us, root us to the present. Let us name where we are. Let us welcome ourselves to the conundrum, the space where all partnerships can happen.

Let us begin our beginning in praise. At the outset let's acknowledge the Patriarch of Resource Sharing, for resource sharing is no less a partnership. The Patriarch of Resource Sharing, John Donne, says, "No man [sic] is an island . . . . no library stands alone." (Translation from the virtual to the virtual ridiculous.)

Without a trace of the ridiculous, in a very rooted way, David Stam states, "Despite the alleged aloofness and elitism of large research libraries, [we] must all realize, no matter what the nature of [our] own institution that all libraries are linked in a great chain of access and that what each has done and does will have importance for the whole universe of libraries and their access."[1]

Returning to the middle muddle: How like the Internet hath our conundrum been to thee. The pleasure of the fleeing search! What freezing ups have we felt, what dark screen seen! What old time's waste everywhere!

Perhaps, it no longer matters as much as it once did, how we got where we are. For where we are changes, and is proportional to our desire to be somewhere else. And that somewhere else is still a conundrum.

I am rarely persuaded solely by the fleshiness of fact. I am, however, frequently persuaded by a particular way of seeing how something relates in qualities to something outside itself. So, why do I hold this conundrum in such fondness? It reminds me of a community of nesting dolls (East European nesting dolls). These dolls are rooted in a culture which can be embraced by other cultures. These are of good design. As Steve Jobs says, good design has to work as well. "Design is a funny word," Jobs says. "Some people think design means how it looks. But of course, if you dig deeper, it's really how it works."[2] Nesting dolls do work well, serving as the ultimate container: the container's container. Nesting dolls are colorful, offer surprise, serendipity, provide the artist latitude to act since nesting dolls can now be found in the form of cats, dogs, and politicians. (Will library directors be next?)

I do not presume to draw an image of a larger entity swallowing a smaller one. We are the sum of the parts of our relationships, of our partnerships. What best describes our situation? We are what we contain; what we are willing to contain, by what we are contained. Like our nesting dolls, our conundrum has a multiplicity of voices; good design is inherent in their healthy partnerships, and, who knows, it is probably Web-enabled.

In a conundrum, opportunities for learning are vast, often quick paced. Proclivity for learning is personal, frequently quixotic. I know something because its qualities remind me of something else. For example, I can describe a serial with quixotic certainty as the Oakland Bay Bridge. It begins in mayhem, goes on for much too long, seldom matches my desired speed, falls off into construction and continues on as something else (i.e., Route 80). All agree the Bay Bridge is falling down; few will agree what it will take to fix it, except lots of money, too much money. One suggested design is to cable it, making it look much like a cathedral. I think the Bay Bridge–as serials in general–can profit from engaging with a Higher Wisdom. Often, I am stalled in traffic on the Bay Bridge, which puts me in the state analogous to claiming. And, of course, there are no free rides.

Opportunities for partnerships are everywhere. However, the conundrum is a seed bed for partnering. Let us look at the proclivities for partnering. Tom Shaughnessy points out that libraries have lived from one crisis to the next.[3] I think libraries are entering one partnership after another: waves of partnerships.

We have reached the space within the conundrum–a certain-sized nesting doll–where we will spend most of our time during this presentation. We will witness four areas: (1) qualities of partnerships, (2) partnerships among vendors and libraries, in particular with collection development issues, (3) the role of the vendor, and (4) a closing comment.

I suggest twelve qualities of partnership:

1. Partnerships are plural. It takes more than one of anything to partner. Partnerships are rooted in community.
2. Partnerships can teach lessons of paradox. Please observe these statements: (1) partnerships offer mutual advantage. I suggest advantage is one-dimensional, moving in one direction. (2) Partnerships are selectively inclusive. Does that mean exclusively inclusive?

3. Partnerships mirror the fractal beauty of physics. Partnerships are dynamic, often colorful, sometimes explosive, often breathtaking.
4. Partnerships are ubiquitous. Is there anything that is not a partnership? Is there anything that was not formerly (at least in parts) a partnership?
5. Partnerships breathe the air of economics, politics, organizations. "Economics and organizational issues often govern our institutional priorities rather than the collecting strengths and cooperative commitments established with such care and effort."[4]
6. Partnerships can be motivated by prestige.
7. Partnerships are more personal than clinical.
8. Partnerships can be experimental. They can be serious play. Beta-testing with a subscription vendor and/or an ILS system are examples of the experimental qualities of partnership. Developing Web pages is both a practical marketing partnership as well as the opportunity to play with the technology to gain future partnerships.
9. Partnerships do not have to change the world to be significant. Steve Jobs offers a balanced perspective: "It's a disservice to constantly put things in this radical new light—that it's going to change everything. Things don't have to change the world to be important."[5]
10. Some partnerships are unwritten, "unspoken," inviolate. These might be fiats from high levels within organizations.
11. Partnerships are mutable. Partnerships can be adjusted, twigged, tweaked, upgraded, downsized, right-sized, outsourced, ignored.
12. Partnerships create vocabulary. The importance of anything can be observed in proportion to the amount of new words it generates. We have well served the concept of re-engineering. I am confident we will partner to the max.

Let us move from the qualities of partnership to our second topic, the kinds of partnerships emerging among vendors and libraries, especially as they relate to collection development and its related family.

I observe 6 such partnerships:

1. *Unmediated partnership.* The Internet is a prime example of unmediated partnership and will probably remain so until it becomes for-profit. Vendors' Web pages are openly accessible. Steve Jobs has a cautionary comment for us on the Web. He does not buy into the Web transforming every person into a publisher. "The heart of the web," Jobs said, "will be commerce, and the heart of commerce will be corporate America serving custom products to individual consumers."[6] Let's gear up when the Web is controlled, inspired or informed by big profits.
2. *Resource sharing.* Resource sharing includes the collection, databases, and avenues to access. On an informal, often ad hoc basis, collection development librarians share ways, methods, policies, with collection development colleagues in other institutions.

    Tony Ferguson underscores the importance of colleagues outside their institution cooperating in particular for materials not supplied by vendors.[7]

    Resource sharing can be geographically based, peer-based, consortial-driven, selective, open, formal, informal. Examples of resources sharing flow from the macro to the micro: from The University of California, ILLINET, OhioLINK to informal partnerships between peer libraries.

    "The institution and the library must maintain the primary collection for their local needs no matter what riches are available to them through resource sharing. The one flaw in all resource sharing assumptions by administrators is the expectation that they will save money. They won't. If there is no collection, you cannot share it. And the aim of resource sharing is to embrace the wealth of the national collection and thereby support and expand the scholarly record for local users." "The collection is still the heart of the matter, and if there is no collection there is nothing to share."[8]

    I offer one aside on document delivery and resource sharing. Inherent in the document delivery system is an anti-resource sharing bias. You can still "own" the sliver of information by accessing it piece-meal. Ownership as defined by possession is then transferred to the requester, or the end-user, not to the traditional library or information cen-

ter. The illusion still holds that someone owns it. Document delivery provides off-site ownership.
3. *Partnerships for hire.* Partnerships can be entered into with outside consultants to review the organization or to undertake specific projects.
4. *Outsourcing.* Outsourcing is a hot topic although applications of outsourcing are not new. The approval plan and consolidated serials check-in services are prime examples of outsourcing. Vendors can manage technical service operations, on-site.
5. *Self or intra-partnering.* This occurs largely in libraries where teams rely on in-house expert partners (i.e., the serials department "contracts" with its assigned expert partner for assistance with vendor software).
6. *Partnerships for obtaining and being advised of materials of interest to the collection.* I find a short summary of the CODES [Collection Development and Evaluation Section] discussion group in COGNOTES to be of interest. "The committee has not discussed collection development concerns for serials. Collection development tends to focus evaluation tools for monographic collections and concentrates on the frequency versus the quality of the collection."[9]

What's the role, the responsibility of a vendor obtaining fringe materials?

Traditionally, vendors have assisted libraries in acquiring core material (largely through approval plan; document delivery). Vendor assistance for fringe material is largely locating publishers for these often esoteric materials. Yet, fringe material is seen as the heart of the library collection. The core collection is the necessity; maybe not exciting, not going to differentiate the library from its competition (i.e., peer libraries).

The fringe of the collection is like the face of a person, what differentiates it, makes it unique, special, worth knowing, worth doing something about, worth protecting, and in the fullest measure, worth being passionate about.

We come to our third area. What is the voice of the vendor in the conundrum? What is the vendor's role? Vendors are conduits, filters, mediators, interpreters, creators, and packagers of information.

Vendors do the following:

- provide routine subscription services
- provide access to a multiplicity of types and formats of information. "The challenge of this generation of librarians is to seamlessly knit together a multiplicity of formats and access mechanisms into one intellectually cohesive, user-friendly set of information resources and services."[10] I prefer the image of quilting. We knit bones, and quilt our diversity, our special strengths, and make them easily available.
- serve as the conduit and filter for publishing information
- provide outsourcing options
- offer access to collection development information
- provide avenue to access, i.e., document delivery, full-text
- provide convenient access to their services and products through their Web page
- offer focus groups for new services, in-house training seminars, and regional service and product seminars on topics of interest
- interface with ILS systems and alpha/beta-test new components
- spearhead industry standards
- act as trainers, consultants, i.e., Internet
- make a profit, have fun.

What is a healthy partnership from a vendor's standpoint? Vendors seek:

- a consistent, fair, and articulated mechanism to review the progress and health of the partnership
- willingness to commit to a long-term partnership (i.e., multi-year)
- partnerships which result in profitability and are perceived as innovational to make the vendor a market leader
- partnerships which contribute to the inherent "goodness" of libraries.

Issues for the vendor are profit stream, market perception, market tolerance, competitive advantage, staff levels and expertise, in-house training issue, long-term and short-term investments. In short, vendors balance, juggle resource needs, market conditions, and return on investment. Vendors look if not to create, at least be aware of and gear up for the "next insanely great thing."[11] Vendors also need to be prepared for the demise of the present insanely great thing and/or its opposite.

There are minimally two ways of asking any question. Phrasing the question in polite circumspection or cutting directly to the quick. For instance, I am asked the same question in two ways, (1) "What is the future of the serials vendor?" (2) "So, vendors are being thrown to the wolves, right?"

There is a role, a present for those vendors with resources to develop, market, and sustain partnerships. To put it another way, vendors who manage their portfolio of partnerships have a higher probability of surviving, of flourishing.

By the way, wolves are smart, they want nothing to do with any of us.

In my most optimistic mood, I associate partnerships in a conundrum with the fresh beauty of the 21-year old Swiss mime trio Mummenshanz. With these exquisite and playful shape-shifters we cannot believe what is unfolding in front of us, even as we see it and begin recognizing the shapes. We are enchanted, transported, possibly made grateful.

A conundrum is a mecca for conversation, for comments, for opinions, not for rigid conclusions. Finally, (trust me) I offer a comment for the close. I suggest we embrace partnerships–if not with overt exuberance–at least in the spirit of the French Little Sparrow, Edith Piaf, with "No Regrets."

NOTES

1. Richard M. Dougherty "A Conceptual Framework for Organizing Resource Sharing and Shared Collection and Development Programs" The Journal of Academic Librarianship 14(5) (November 1, 1988) p. 189.

2. Gary Wolf The Wired Interview "Steve Jobs: The Next Insanely Great Thing" WIRED 4.02 (February 1996) p. 163.

3. Thomas W. Shaughnessy "Resource Sharing and the End of Innocence" in Access, Ownership, and Resource Sharing, Sul Lee, editor. (Binghamton, NY: The Haworth Press, Inc., 1994), p. 3.

4. Gay N. Dannelly "Resource Sharing in the Electronic Era: Potentials and Paradoxes," LIBRARY TRENDS 43(4) (Spring 1995) p. 666.

5. Ibid. WIRED, p. 107.

6. Ibid., 102.

7. Anthony Ferguson "Document Delivery in the Electronic Age: Collecting and Service Implications," reported by Rachel Miller, Access, Resource Sharing, and Collection Development, Library Acquisitions: Practice and Theory 19(4) (1995) p. 482.

8. Ibid, Dannelly, p. 677.

9. Rosanne E. Trujillo, "Collection Evaluation Techniques Initiative Investigated" COGNOTES Wrapup Issue, p. 8.

10. Samuel Demas "Collection Development for the Electronic Library: A Conceptual and Organizational Model" Library Hi Tech 12(3) 1994, p. 72.

11. Ibid., WIRED, taken from the title, cover page.

New Partners for Collection Development

Rebecca T. Lenzini

INTRODUCTION

The number of information providers in the electronic environment is increasing: the Gale *Directory of Databases* now lists roughly 10,000 databases from 3,500 database producers and offered by 810 online services. Yet this number pales in comparison when we consider the millions of computers and servers on the Internet, many of which are vending products and services using the World Wide Web and other networking technologies. Indeed, today anyone with a home PC can truly become a database producer.

What were once separate roles of collection development and database selection are, of necessity, merging: as more and more providers offer full text and complete information delivery options, collection developers of necessity must play a larger and larger role in the selection, acquisition and continued development of these services. Collection developers must now work with not only the familiar faces of book vendors and subscription agents, but also with indexing and abstracting services, various types of aggregators of information, local system vendors who increasingly offer information services, publishers who are pushing WEB locations and even services aimed squarely at the library's end users.

Rebecca T. Lenzini is President of CARL Corporation in Denver, CO.

Much of the information contained in this report is based on an internal study completed for the CARL Corporation. The author wishes to acknowledge with gratitude that study's compiler: George Machovec.

[Haworth co-indexing entry note]: "New Partners for Collection Development." Lenzini, Rebecca T. Co-published simultaneously in *Journal of Library Administration* (The Haworth Press, Inc.) Vol. 24, No. 1/2, 1996, pp. 113-124; and: *Emerging Patterns of Collection Development in Expanding Resource Sharing, Electronic Information and Network Environment* (ed: Sul H. Lee) The Haworth Press, Inc., 1996, pp. 113-124. Single or multiple copies of this article are available for a fee from The Haworth Document Delivery Service [1-800-342-9678, 9:00 a.m. - 5:00 p.m. (EST). E-mail address: getinfo@haworth.com].

© 1996 by The Haworth Press, Inc. All rights reserved.

In this paper, I'd like to briefly review the developments of the past few years which have led us to our current position and then to categorize and describe the present assortment of information providers who are deserving of the attention of collection development professionals. To illustrate both trends and current categories of providers, I will frequently mention specific corporations and/or products; however, my survey is intended to be illustrative only and not inclusive. Finally, the paper will conclude with a summary of recent trends and issues which will likely affect collection development decisions in the future.

TRADITIONAL ROLES

The task of the collection development professional has traditionally been to allocate the library's financial resources in as effective a manner as possible toward the acquisition of materials in support of the larger institution's goals. Typically, collection developers have worked to acquire books, journals, media, and other materials in support of academic programs, research initiatives, and past commitments (to subject areas, to special disciplines, special collections, etc.).

Sharing of materials has always been relevant to collection developers who have, over the years, attempted to characterize their various collection strengths to facilitate resource sharing, using tools such as the RLG conspectus, or other methods. In recent years, interlibrary loan and circulation statistics have become even more important to those responsible for building the collection, since, as resources have become tighter, it has become even more important to understand what is actually used and what can be acquired "just in time" through services such as document delivery or interlibrary loan.

When it comes to database selection, choices traditionally have been made by committees of public service or reference personnel. These staff members select from the thousands of available databases typically in a variety of electronic formats and access methods, including CD-ROMs, online services, locally mounted databases, or gateways to host systems.

To date, there has been an important, implied difference in the activities of these two groups: database selectors have dealt with citation level or secondary access tools; collection developers with the acquisition of primary material.

Naturally, the two groups have also had different vendor contacts in the industry: database selectors traditionally work with Indexing & Abstracting (I&A) services (such as IAC, UMI, etc.), with CD-ROM providers (such as SilverPlatter, OVID, etc.) or with online providers (such as DIALOG, OCLC FirstSearch, etc.); collection developers have dealt with book vendors (such as BNA, Midwest, Yankee, etc.) or subscription agents (such as Dawson/Faxon, EBSCO, Swets, Harrassowitz, BHB, etc.).

CHANGES FROM THE EARLY 1990s

One of the events which altered the traditional collection development and database landscape was the emergence of what were called CASIAS services (a term more popular in the UK than in the US) which stands for "Current Awareness Service–Individual Article Supply." UnCover, which began offering document delivery beginning in 1991, was the first service of this kind which combined a citation level database with a document delivery service. UnCover was followed by others such as the EBSCO/BLDSC Inside Information partnership, the Faxon Finder and, somewhat later, UMI's ABI/Power Pages combination (and more recently UMI's ProQuest and ProQuest Direct services). Of note, these combinations of databases and document delivery, while clearly offering database selectors another choice for citation level access, were actually of more immediate interest to collection developers because of their ties to document delivery and primary content.

Meanwhile, in the same period, I&A providers were moving away from CD-ROM-based systems to more online options to take advantage of the wide-spread growth of library systems and networks. These providers continued to work with database selectors, but increasingly found themselves dealing with local system vendors. Early trends favored local loading of databases on systems such as NOTIS, GEAC, DRA and CARL.

Patrons quickly learned to love the "anytime, anywhere" access which these expanded online library systems provided, but they also expressed their frustration at citation-only access and made clear their need for more and more of the "real thing" or the primary data. In response, I&As moved rapidly to gear up to provide more and more full-text options.

At the same time, libraries learned the financial and human resource burden of locally loaded options—high hardware costs, high human resource costs, high maintenance overall—and even more so when full-text was added. As an example, consider that CARL by itself now devotes 25 gigabytes to IAC data alone and another 12 gigabytes to UMI data.

In fact, it was in response to just these factors and needs that I&A services and local system vendors partnered to offer the first "gateway" services for their clients, taking on the burden of loading and updating the massive citation and full-text databases. DRAnet, Ameritech/Dynix VISTA, Innovative's INNview and the CARL Database Shopping List are examples of vendor gateways in use today which first appeared in the early 1990s. While these gateways are available for use by virtually any library, most users of the services are also users of the vendor's integrated library system (ILS) who are taking advantage of the same search interface for both the library's catalog and desired information databases.

Bibliographic utilities also moved to address the challenge of providing easier access to database information for their customers and users, with OCLC's FirstSearch and RLG's Citadel service appearing in roughly this same time frame.

CURRENT MODELS

Most of the gateways referenced above provide not only database access but also full-text files or other document delivery links. OCLC and RLG also provide links to ILL. So all of these gateways can be thought of as offering one current model for combined database access and document delivery. A number of other models also exist, some of which are new to the library market and may not be well known at this time. For the purposes of this paper, we'll examine six other models, giving brief descriptions of each and examples of current providers.

First Model: I&A Host or Gateway Services

During the past two years, several major I&A services have established their own host-based gateways for access to their major databases, and in some cases, even other producer's databases. The primary advantage to this approach for these database producers is increased control over their product, including the currency of the data, the search interface, and the validation of users. The downside for the library user is the need to master yet another searching protocol. Obvious examples of this model include:

- EBSCOhost . . . which offers, primarily, access to the EBSCO family of citation databases, as well as the BLDSC table of contents file.
- IAC's InfoTrac Searchbank . . . which provides access to a growing number of popular IAC databases, as well as other files including PsycINFO.
- UMI's ProQuest Direct . . . which offers access to a suite of UMI databases as well as other services.

UnCover most likely fits best into this model, since it has always been hosted by its "I&A" creator, CARL. UnCover remains the largest single citation database linked to document delivery, with over 17,000 individual titles and now over 8,000,000 citations in the database.

Of the four "host" services in the examples, most now offer, or will soon offer, graphical clients, WEB interfaces, and Z39.50 support. Ironically, one of the real challenges and potential limitations of the new I&A gateway services is their ability to support the wide range of dumb terminals found throughout libraries. Collection developers who make plans to incorporate these services into the standard package of offerings must take care to learn exactly which devices and network connections on campus are compatible.

Second Model: Networked CD-ROM/Servers

Standalone CD-ROMs are still a popular medium for home use and low-use library files, but many libraries have moved rapidly to locally loading these pre-mastered databases on file servers or even gatewaying to commercial services from traditional CD-ROM distributors. At least two major CD-ROM distributors are now offering products and services which facilitate this move:

- OVID Technologies . . . has traditionally combined its search engine with biomedical and other scientific databases and now offers a UNIX-based version for local networked access.
- SilverPlatter . . . began development in 1993 of its Electronic Reference Library (ERL) concept in which databases could be offered in a wide area network or through the Internet via a UNIX-based server. The product was released late in 1994. Databases on ERL may be loaded either on hard disk for high use levels or CD-ROM for low use levels in any mix.

Both of these services offer links to document delivery services, OVID via Medline, primarily, as well as through full-text; SilverPlatter via UnCover, among others.

Third Model: "Aggregated" Options

In the category of very new approaches are services which load primary information of a variety of types into a single file for "one stop" searching. At least two new entrants in this category are aiming at the K-12 and undergraduate level user:

- Infonautics' Electric Library . . . appeared on Prodigy in the spring of 1995 and now is also available via the WEB, as well as on the Microsoft Network and Apple's eWorld service. Electric Library combines natural language searching with a single database of full-text articles from 900 magazines, over 100 newspapers, two encyclopedias, dictionaries, reference books and other monographs, including Cliffs Notes, Shakespeare and the Bible, two news feeds, media transcripts as well as photo archives and maps.
- IAC's Cognito . . . has been developed by its Consumer Division. This web-based product offers access to a combined set of resources similar to those offered by Electric Library. The product is initially being targeted to end-users in their homes.

Both these services are aimed squarely at end-users, as is evidenced by their inclusion of ONLY full-text sources combined with natural language (non-library) type searching. Electric Library is presently being offered to libraries through re-seller agreements (CARL is re-selling to public libraries) and IAC has announced its intention to offer Cognito to the library market.

Fourth Model: "Targeted" Options

Perhaps the opposite of the general-use services described above, some providers are introducing database products which are aimed at very targeted user segments. Examples from CARL's new parent company, Knight Ridder Information, Inc. include:

- ProBase . . . a client interface to DIALOG and DataStar for professional searchers and information retrievers.
- BusinessBase . . . a windows client which accesses selected financial and company profile data.
- ScienceBase . . . a WEB interface which offers subscription-based access to combined index and abstract files, with links for document delivery.

Another example provided by a subsidiary of SilverPlatter is:

- Physicians' Home Page . . . a WEB-based targeted index to materials of interest to medical practitioners, with links for document delivery.

Like Cognito and Electric Library, these products are aimed squarely at end-user information consumers, though clearly of a different type.

Fifth Model: Publishers on the WEB

More and more primary publishers and learned societies are now offering Home Pages which provide both citation level information as well as full articles from their publications. Rather than offer specific examples of publisher pages, in this case a few observations are in order:

- Title orientation . . . most of the services I have viewed work very well for the user who is tracking a particular title, its table of contents, etc.
- Trials are limited . . . online registration for free-trial access works very well, but it is rare that a full article can be accessed during a trial. Citations and abstracts are more likely to be available.
- Forthcoming listings . . . several services feature lists of forthcoming articles, or even articles under consideration, a very helpful service.

All in all, these services appear to be well designed, graphically pleasing and they offer very useful information, in addition to the publications data itself. They will undoubtedly serve narrow use very successfully. However, the user who is researching a field of knowledge will need to begin with a broader tool of some type, typically a citation index or TOC database, before branching to these services.

Sixth Model: Printers and Others on the WEB

The move to digitize and offer primary information on the WEB is actually so widespread that no one could hope to describe the field in a short paper. A number of printers or others who provide services to journal publishers have very interesting offerings now up and running. Several examples are worth noting:

- CatchWord . . . is both an electronic journals conversion product and a management service, which now houses Taylor & Francis and Carfax articles, among others. CatchWord uses multiple servers geographically distributed to manage online article access and distribution, and through its proprietary formats handles security in ways which publishers will find comforting.
- JSTOR . . . a project undertaken by the Mellon Foundation is digitizing ten core scholarly journals in the fields of economics and history—including the *American Economic Review* and the *American Historical Review.* JSTOR anticipates distributing copies of this electronic "collection" to interested libraries.

- CADMUS Digital Solutions ... with its "Journals.At-Home" service provides an Internet "host" service for journals published by the American Heart Association, the American Society for Investigative Pathology, the American Society of Microbiology, as well as the *Journal of Immunology*. According to a press release issued at International Online in December 1995, issues on the service go on-line simultaneously with the mailing of printed copies. Document delivery links to UnCover have been announced to fulfill article orders for back issues or for those articles which are not yet in digital form.

And, of course, a true seventh model exists and that is of authors loading their own works and making them available through personal servers on the network. In the world of scholarly publishing, this model appears to be used primarily to facilitate speedy distribution of information for comment and general sharing, with traditional publication still playing its archival and quality-stamping role. However, as we have discussed before at this meeting, the trend of authors taking back control is a definite one.

TRENDS

In considering the models presented, however, the general move is clearly to link secondary references to full text/primary information in all environments. Many of the services noted in the examples provide links from a database or service to a document supplier such as UnCover or UMI. This year, users should begin to see the flip side of the equation; that is, links from services such as UnCover to the distributed locations of the full-text article or image, on publisher servers, printer servers or even author servers.

In this coming model, databases like UnCover become "whole earth article catalogs" which contain the necessary pointers to link users automatically to the primary information they seek, with the advantage over a publisher server, for example, of being able to supply users with documents retrieved from multiple locations rather than only one.

One major technical trend of importance on the database access side is the growing support of the Z39.50 protocols. With very few exceptions, most of the services mentioned already provide Z39.50 client/server compliance which has the net effect of eliminating any interface barriers which may have marred the user's success of access. An old rule of computing says that "information = data + interface"; widespread compliance with Z39.50 helps simplify this basic equation.

Z39.50 is also coming into play in another area of particular importance to collection developers: links to holdings from these various database services. Particularly at the citation level, a link to holdings allows the library to make maximum use of its collection and the investment made in that collection. Most services offering holdings links now require some type of re-loading or re-keying. Using Z39.50, one service (OVID) already makes "calls" to the library's catalog and retrieves holdings statements which are current and therefore of greatest use.

On the business side, another trend is clear: partnering with or acquiring full service document delivery operations. Notice EBSCO's purchase of Dynamic Information, UMI's purchase of Information Store and KRII's purchase of UnCover as a partner for its Source-One service. All of these moves are designed to position these providers to offer library or other customers "full service" document supply for anything required. Ironically, though some like SourceOne and UMI are building up digitized collections, most of these operations are dependent on library collections for the bulk of their fulfillment, a fact which is not likely to change soon.

ISSUES FOR COLLECTION DEVELOPERS

Certainly, the first issue must be simply "how to keep up" amidst all these developments (or perhaps, "how to catch up" and become not just a collection developer but also a database selector!). Indeed, how to evaluate and position all these options, in addition to traditional published material, presents a challenge even for the talents of the Chuck Hamakers and Tony Fergusons of the field.

It is my opinion that those of us who are in a position to create and offer new services which help make the acquisition of primary information less fragmented will be in a strong position, as the choices are likely to continue to multiply exponentially.

A related challenge appears to be how collection developers will differentiate and address equitably the needs of undergraduates and researchers (faculty, graduate students, etc.) in the new environment, where both sectors will be the targets of a number of end-user oriented services such as Cognito or Electric Library for the undergraduate, and ScienceBase for the researcher. Perhaps it will devolve to every man for himself, based on what each can afford. Yet the library will need to determine how best to serve its role as equalizer in this area of service provision.

Pricing will undoubtedly continue to be a major issue. Three models seem to be emerging for the various components of the online article or record (the citation, the abstract and the full-text or image): transaction based, licensed/subscription, or concurrent use based. It is my opinion that pricing is generally moving in the right direction, with many services now offering combinations of these algorithms which can be "mixed and matched" to best serve a given institution's pattern of use.

Finally, the issue of copyright is one which will remain of paramount importance as our use of online information increases. In addition to the obvious legal implications, copyright has an immediate impact on pricing. Today, some suppliers with special copyright or intellectual property agreements with publishers are able to deliver huge numbers of articles at low costs. But these very agreements are under debate and pressure from a number of sources, including the authors themselves, who are concerned that they will be left behind in the brave new online world. It is important for us as professionals in the information industry to work for equitable and fair compensation for rights holders, while ensuring our ability to make information as widely available as possible.

The pace of change is rapid, but the opportunities for improved access for our users to the world of information are real. Collection developers are uniquely positioned to bring both qualitative and quantitative decision skills to the table. In working with your new partners in collection development, never forget that your influence will help to shape this entire industry during this next critical period.

FURTHER READING

Readers can find more information on many of the companies, organizations or services named in this paper at the following WEB addresses:

BNA	http://www.blackwell.com
Cadmus	http://www.cadmus.com
CARL and UnCover	http://www.carl.org
CatchWord	http://www.catchword.co.uk
COGNITO	http://www.cognito.com
DRA	http://www.dra.com
Dynix/Ameritech	http://www.amlibs.com
EBSCO	http://www.ebsco.com
Elsevier	http://www.elsevier.com
Faxon	http://www.faxon.com
GEAC	http://www.geac.com
IAC	http://www.iacnet.com
III	http://www.iii.com
Infonautics	http://www.infonautics.com
JSTOR	http://www.lib.umich.edu/libhome/jstorsumm.html
John Wiley & Sons	http://www.wiley.com
Knight Ridder/Dialog	http://www.dialog.com
National Writers Union	http://www.igc.apc.org/nwu/
OCLC	http://www.oclc.org
OVID	http://www.ovid.com
Physicians' Home Page	http://www.silverplatter.com/physicians/index.html
RLG	http://www.rlg.org
Silverplatter	http://www.silverplatter.com
UMI	http://www.umi.com
Z39.50 information	http://lcweb.loc.gov/z3950/agency/

Index

Academic departments, purchase of research materials by, 23
Academic libraries
 budgets, 49-50
 lack of funding for, 48-49
American Airlines, 23,25
American Association of Universities, 13,66
American Economic Review, 120
American Express charge card, 21-22, 23,24,25-27,29-30,31-32
American Heart Association journals, 121
American Historical Review, 120
American Journal of Microbiology, 121
American Library Association
 Interlibrary Communications and Information Networks conference, 55-56
 interlibrary cooperative policy statement, 56
American Memory project, 99,100
American Society for Investigative Pathology journals, 121
Ameritech/Dynix, 116,124
Andrew Mellon Foundation, J-STOR Project, 68,120,124
Apple, eWorld service, 118
Archiving, of electronic journals, 9
Area studies
 cooperative microform projects in, 61
 coordinated collective development in, 58
ARIEL, 60,61
Association of Research Libraries (ARL)
 book purchases decrease by, 36
 Chesapeake Information and Research Library Alliance participation, 54,65
 cooperative cataloging program, 56-57
 foreign acquisitions program, 13, 66,97
 library use trends of, 22-23
 resource sharing coordination by, 66,67
 serials subscriptions of, 36
Associations, as academic periodicals publishers, 78, 79
Australia
 Distributed National Collection, 66
 National Bibliographic Database, 91
 National Library, 90-91,92
Australian Libraries Summit, 91
Authors, use of World Wide Web by, 121

Beowulf, electronic version of, 91-92
BHB, 115
Bibliographic utilities
 gateway services of, 116
 library subscriptions to, 50
Biblioteka Narodowa, 88-89
Big Ten research libraries, resource sharing by, 14-15,59-60
Billington, James H., 96,98
BLDS Institute Information/EBSCO partnership, 115,117
BNA, 115,124
Book vendors, 115

Boston Library Consortium, 59,63, 64,65-66,67,69,70
Boston Public Library, 59
Boston University, 59
Brady, Matthew, 99
Brand extension, 26-29
British Library, *Strategic Objectives of*, 91-92
Brittanica products, purchase by consortia, 59
Brown University Library, 59,65
  budget, 49-50,51
  NELINET use by, 69
Bucknell University, Bertrand Library multimedia collection, 27-28
Budgets, for electronic services, 51, 53-54
Buffet, Warren, 32
Burleson, Omar, 94
BusinessBase, 119

CADMUS, 121,124
Canada
  National Librarian, 89,90
  National Library, 88,89-90,92
CARL, 51,115,116,117,119,124
CASIAS (current awareness service-individual article supply), 115
Cataloging
  of the Internet, 67-68
CatchWord, 120,124
CD-ROMs
  libraries' purchase of, 49
  in multimedia collections, 27-28
  networked, 117-118
  providers of, 115
Center for Research Libraries, 61, 63,67
Chesapeake Information and Research Library Alliance (CIRLA), 54,65
Citadel, 116

Clinton, Bill, 19-20
Closed-loop systems, 30-32
Co-branding, 25-26
COGNITO, 118-119,123,124
COGNOTES, Collection Development and Evaluation Section (CODES) of, 108
Collection developers, traditional roles, 114-115
Collection development
  collaborative, 58-59
  coordinated, 58
  decision-making in, 24
  electronic services for, 113-124
    "aggregated" options, 118-119
    indexing and abstracting host-based gateways, 116, 117
    issues in, 122-123
    networked CD-ROM/servers, 117-118
    publishers and printers on World Wide Web, 119-121
    "targeted" options, 119
    trends in, 121-122
  national system, 66
  policies for, 8-11
    effect of digitization on, 4,9
    effect of managed information on, 11-16
Collections
  cost-effectiveness of, 20-21
  fringe material of, 108
  homogeneity of, 3-4
Commission on Preservation and Access, 99
Committee on Interinstitutional Cooperation, 59-60
Commonwealth Parliamentary Library, Australia, 90
Community colleges, resource sharing by, 62
Confidentiality, of library patrons' records, 31-32

Consortia. *See also* specific consortia
   cost sharing by, 59
   resource sharing by, 54
Cooperative holdings agreements,
      59,64
Copyright
   of electronic information, 56,
      99-100,123
   violations of, actionable evidence
      against, 79
Copyright Act of 1870, 94
Copyright fee, for article databases,
      52-53
Cornell University, 57
Council on Library Resources, 67
Credit cards, 21-22,23,24,25-27,
      29-30,31,32
Current awareness service-individual
      article supply (CASIAS),
      115
Current Contents, 26
Databases. *See also* names of
      specific databases
   number of available, 113
   selection of, 113,114-115
DataStar, 119
Dawson/Faxon, 115
Decision-making, in collection
      development, 24
Delta Air Lines SkyMiles card,
      25-26,27
Detroit Publishing Company, 99
DIALOG, 115,119
Digital Library, of Library of
      Congress, 68
Digitization, 10-11
   impact on collection development
      policies, 4,9
   by Library of Congress, 98-100
   of manuscripts, 91-92
   versus paper-based material, 6-7
Directory of Databases, 113
Distance education, 11,15-16
Distance information, 3-17. *See also*
      Electronic services

impact on collection development
      policies, 8-11
   as managed information, 11-16
DOC-LINE, 68
Document delivery services, 4,51
   article indexes of, 68
   of CADMUS Digital Solutions,
      121
   CD-ROM access to, 118
   cooperative, 62-63,67
   copyright fees for, 52-53
   as current-awareness-individual
      article supply, 115
   limitations of, 52-53
   relationship to resource sharing,
      107-108
   as substitute for serials
      subscriptions, 51,82
Donne, John, 104
DRA, 115,116,124
Duke University, 58
Dutch Centre for Library Automation
      (PICA), 62-63,67
Dynamic Information, 122
Dynix/Ameritech, 116,124

EBSCO, 115,122,124
EBSCO/BLDSC Inside Information
      partnership, 115,117
EBSCO/doc, 51
EBSCOhost, 117
Electric Library, 118-119,123
"Electronic *Beowulf*," 91-92
Electronic data
   access to, 48
   copyright of, 56,99-100,123
Electronic Libraries Project, 92-93
Electronic mail, 50-51,60
Electronic resource centers, regional,
      61
Electronic services, 50-55
   advantages of, 51-52
   budgets for, 51,53-54
   for collection development,
      113-124

"aggregated" options, 118-119
indexing and abstracting
   host-based gateways,
     116,117
   issues in, 122-123
   networked CD-ROM/servers,
     117-118
   printers and publishers on
     World Wide Web, 119-121
   "targeted" options, 119
   trends in, 121-122
cost of, 51,52,53-54
definition of, 50
equipment required for, 52
librarians' misconceptions about, 64-65
national libraries' use of, 91-93
resource sharing of, 55-70
   characteristics of, 63-64
   computer compatibility in, 56, 57
   expansion of, 64-66
   historical perspective on, 55-57
   obstacles to, 55-56
   recommendations for, 66-70
   types of, 50-51
supplemental nature of, 53
Elsevier, 37,124
E-mail, 50-51,60
Encarta Encyclopedia, 27
Esposito, Joseph P., 59

Farmington Plan, 13,57,66
FAUL (Five Associated University Libraries) organization, 57,65
Faxon, 124
Faxon/Dawson, 115
Faxon Finder, 115
Federal Communication Commission (FCC), 55
Ferguson, Tony, 122
File servers, CD-ROM databases on, 117-118

FIRN (Florida Information Resources Network), 62
FirstSearch, 98,115,116
Five Associated University Libraries (FAUL) organization, 57,65
Florida Information Resources Network (FIRN), 62
Focus groups, of vendors, 109
Fringe material, 108

GALILEO, 59
Gateway services, 116-117
GEAC, 115,124
General Motors, 23
Georgetown University, 54
German, Charles, 64-65
Germany, special libraries system of, 66
Greater Midwest Research Library Consortium (GMRLC), 62
Group of Seven, Electronic Libraries Project, 92-93

Hamaker, Charles, 122
Harrassowitz, 115
Harvard University, 57
Higher Education Act of 1965, 56-57
Hill, Lister, 93-94
Holdings data
   cooperative agreements regarding, 59,64
   coordination of, 68-69
   retrieval of, 122
Howard University, 54
Hypertext, 5

IAC, 115,116,124
   COGNITO, 118-119,123,124
   InfoTrac Searchband, 117
ILLINET, 107
Impact Factor, 80-81
Indexing, of document delivery articles, 68

Indexing and abstracting services, 50
    gateway services, 116,117
    online, 113,115-116
Infonautics, 118-119,124
Information management
    organizations (IMOs), 13, 15
Information Society Summit 1995, 92-93
Information Store, 122
Information technology. *See also* Electronic services
    economic impact of, 49
    impact on libraries, 19-20
        public opinion about, 22
    impact on universities, 5,10-11
    projected trends in, 47-48
InfoTrac Searchband, 117
INNview, 116
Institute for Scientific Information
    Impact Factor, 80-81
Interlibrary Communications and Information Networks conference, 55-56
Interlibrary loan, 22
    common, 60
    by medical libraries, 68
    by national libraries, 91
    OCLC links to, 60,116
    Research Libraries Group links to, 116
    user-initiated, 69
Internet, 9. *See also* World Wide Web (WWW)
    cataloging of, 67-68
    cost of, 64
    databases on, 113
    fee for, 51
    library access to, 50
    resource selection for, 9,10
    as unmediated partnership, 107
    verification of information resources on, 68
Interpretive skills, of librarians, 20

Japan, National Diet Library of, 90
Johns Hopkins University, 54
John Wiley & Sons, 124
Journal of Academic Librarianship, 53
Journal of Microbiology, 121
Journals. *See* Serials
J-STOR project, 68,120,124

Kennedy, John F., 93-94
Kluwer, 62-63
Knight Ridder/Dialog, 124
Knight Ridder Information, Inc., 119
KRII, 122

LALINC (Louisiana Academic Library Information Network Consortium), 62
Latin American Cooperative Acquisitions Program (LACAP), 13
Librarians
    interpretive and mediation skills of, 20
    relevance of, 7-8,19-20
Librarianship, "doomsday scenario" of, 19-20
Libraries, as closed-loop systems, 30-32
Library Information Network for Community Colleges (LINCC), 62
Library of Congress, 94-100
    American Memory project, 99,100
    collection policy of, 95-96,97-98
    as de facto national library, 94
    Digital Library of, 68
    electronic technology use by, 98-100
    functions of, 94-95
    funding of, 96-97,98
    as National Library of Australia model, 90

National Program for
    Acquisitions and
    Cataloging, 56-57
  serial collections reduction by,
    97-98
LINCC (Library Information
    Network for Community
    Colleges), 62
Lincoln, Abraham, 93
LOUIS (Louisiana Online University
    Information System),
    62,63,65
Louisiana Academic Library
    Information Network
    Consortium (LALINC), 62
Louisiana Online University
    Information Center
    (LOUIS), 62,63,65
Louisiana State University, serials
    collection cost-effectiveness
    plan, 35-46
  archival considerations, 37
  cancellations, 35,36,40,43
  copyright costs, 40,42
  document delivery services, 38
  journal articles orders, 40-43
  as library-wide plan, 35-36
  new titles acquisition, 43-45
  science faculty survey of, 36-46
  utility cost, 39-40

MacLeish, Archibald, 95-96
MacMillan, Ernest, 92
Managed information, 9,11-16
Manuscripts, digitization of, 91-92
Marketing, of library collections,
    24-32
  brand extension technique, 26-29
  co-branding technique, 25-26
  market segmentation technique,
    29-32
"Marketing of Libraries and
    Information Services," 25
Market segmentation, 29-32

Massachusetts Institute of
    Technology, 59
MasterCard credit card, 21-22,27,
    29-30
Maxwell, Robert, 79
McChesney, John, 28
McKinley, William, 99
Mediation skills, of librarians, 20
Medical libraries, 66,68,118
Medline, 118
Michigan State University, 62,65
Microform projects, in area studies,
    61
Microsoft, *Encarta Encyclopedia*, 27
Microsoft Network, 118
Midwest (book vendor), 115
Midwest Library Center, 61
MIME (Multipurpose Internet Mail
    Extensions), 60
"Mining Automated Systems for
    Collection Management"
    (Atkins), 30
M-Link, 62
*Molecular Crystals and Liquid
    Crystals*, 44
"Morning Edition" (radio show), 28
Multimedia collections, 27-29
Multipurpose Internet Mail
    Extensions (MIME), 60

National Academy of Sciences, 55
National Advisory Commission on
    Libraries, 94
National Agricultural Library, 93,97
National Commission on Libraries
    and Information Science, 55
National Digital Library Federation,
    99
National Endowment for the
    Humanities, Challenge
    grants of, 61
National imprints, as national
    libraries' collection focus,
    87,88
  of Library of Congress, 94,95

of National Library of Australia, 91
of National Library of Canada, 88,89
of National Library of Poland, 88-89
National libraries, 87-101
  collection policies and goals of, 88-91,95-96
  electronic technology use by, 91-93
  foreign materials collection function of, 88-90
National Library of Australia, 90-91, 92
National Library of Canada, 88, 89-90,92
National Library of Medicine, 93-94, 97
National Library of New Zealand, 92
National Library of Poland (Biblioteka Narodowa), 88-89
National Program for Acquisitions and Cataloging (NPAC), 13,56-57
National Science Foundation, 55
National Shelf List Measurement Project, 9
National Writers Union, 124
NELINET, 69
Netherlands
  periodical publishers, 78
  Royal Library, 92
Newman, John Cardinal, 10
New York State research libraries, cooperative preservation fund, 65
North Carolina Central University, 65
North Carolina State University, 58
NOTIS, 62,115

OCLC
  FirstSearch, 98,115,116
  interlibrary loan links of, 60,116
  Internet cataloging by, 67-68
  World Wide Web address, 124
OhioLINK, 60,69,107
On-line public access catalogs (OPAC), 50,62,63
Online searches, cost of, 52
Online systems, common or linked, 61-62
Organic Act, 93
Outsourcing, 108
OVID Technologies, 115,118,122, 124

Page charges, for serials, 80
Paper-based material, 3
  versus digital-formatted material, 6-7
Patron records, privacy and confidentiality of, 31-32
Pergamon, 37
Photograph collections, 92,99
Physicians' Home Page, 124
Piaf, Edith, 110
PICA, 62-63,67
Preservation, 9,99
Price history evaluation
  of academic serials, 73-85
    as basis for cost-containment strategies, 81-85
  of discriminatory pricing, 79-80
  by impact factor, 80-81
  by page charges, 80
  by parent country of publisher, 77-78
  by publisher type, 78-79
  by subject, 77
  of online articles and records, 123
Printers' services, on World Wide Web, 120-121
Privacy, of library patrons' records, 31-32
ProBase, 119
Prodigy, 118
Public Law 480 Program, 13

Public libraries
　increasing use of, 22
　users of, 25
Publishers. *See also* names of
　　individual publishers
　World Wide Web home pages,
　　119-120
Purchasing, consortial, 69

Reference tools, electronic, 51-52,
　118
Research Libraries Group (RLG)
　ARIEL, 60,61
　Citadel service, 116
　Conspectus, 9
　cooperative document delivery
　　service, 62-63,67
　World Wide Web address, 124
Research Triangle University
　Libraries, 58,62,63,65,69
Resource sharing, 26,104
　as collection development
　　component, 9,114
　definition of, 57-58
　of electronic services, 55-70
　　characteristics of, 63-64
　　expansion of, 64-66
　　historical perspective on,
　　　55-57
　　obstacles to, 55-56
　　recommendations for, 66-70
　　types of, 50-51
　factors affecting success of, 69-70
　global, 92-93
　as managed information, 11-16
　by national libraries, 90
　relationship to document delivery
　　services, 107-108
　types of
　　collaborative collection
　　　development, 58-59
　　common interlibrary loan, 60
　　common linked online
　　　systems, 61-62

　　consortial cost sharing, 59
　　consortial sharing of electronic
　　　resources, 59-60
　　cooperative holdings
　　　agreements, 59
　　cooperative or linked storage,
　　　60-61
　　coordinated collective
　　　development, 58
*Responsive Public Library
　Collection: How to Develop
　and Market It* (Baker), 25
Retrospective conversion, to
　electronic form, 68
Royal Library of the Netherlands, 92

Schwengel, Fred, 94
ScienceBase, 119,123
Science Translation Journal Pilot
　Project, 58-59
Scott, Marianne, 89,93
Serials. *See also* titles of specific serials
　cancellation of, 54
　as cost increase factor, 82-83
　faculty support for, 82
　by Library of Congress, 97-99
　cost of. *See also* Price history
　　evaluation, of academic
　　serials
　increase of, 36,40
　library-publisher agreements
　　regarding, 83-85
　last copy titles, 67
　replacement with document
　　delivery services, 51,82
Shared Collections and Access
　Program (SCAP), 58-59
SilverPlatter, 115,118,124
Smithsonian Institution, 54
Societies
　as publishers of academic serials,
　　78,79
　World Wide Web Home Pages of,
　　119
SourceOne, 122

Spofford, Ainsworth Rand, 94
Stanford University, 58-59,63,65
State University of New York, 57
Stewart, Martha, 27
Storage
   cooperative or shared, 60-61,63
   coordinated, 67
   cost-effectiveness of, 65
Swets, 115
Syracuse University, 57

Teleconferencing, 10-11
Texas Council of State University
   Librarians, 14
Texas Higher Education
   Coordinating Board, 14
TexShare, 14,59,63
"Tomorrow Librarian, The"
   (Billings), 19-20
Translation journals, 58-59
Tulane University, 58

UnCover, 37,53,115,117,118,121, 122,124
United Kingdom
   National Central Lending Library, 66
   periodical publishers, 78
U.S. Department of Agriculture
   Library, 93,97
U.S. Office of Education, Bureau of
   Libraries and Educational
   Technology, 55
U.S. Office of Telecommunications
   Policy, 55
University of Delaware, 54
Universities. *See also* names of
   specific universities
   economic crises of, 48-49
   impact of information technology
     on, 5,10-11
University Microfilm International
   (UMI), 51,115,116,122
   database gateways of, 115-117
   document delivery services of, 115
   World Wide Web address log, 124
University of California, 107
   Northern Regional Facility, 61
   resource sharing with Stanford
     University, 58-59,63,65
University of Chicago, 59-60
University of Maryland, 54
University of Massachusetts at
   Amherst, 59
University of Michigan, 62,65
University of North Carolina-Chapel
   Hill, 58
University of Rochester, 57
University of Texas System libraries,
   managed information
   service programs, 14
University of Virginia, 58

Vatican Library, 92
Vendors
   of books, 115
   gateway services, 116-117
   local system, 113,115,116
   partnerships with libraries, 26, 103-111
     qualities of, 105-106
     types of, 106-108
     vendors' roles in, 108-110
   product reporting features of, 30-31
   World Wide Web Home Pages of, 107,109
Virtual library, 52
Virtual Library of Virginia (VIVA), 59,61,64,65
VISA credit card, 21-22,27,29-30
VIVA (Virtual Library of Virginia), 59,61,64,65

"Warning: Information Technology
   Will Transform the
   University" (Wulf), 5

Wayne State University, 62,65
WebCat, 62
WebDOC, 62-63,67
Word processing software, libraries'
    provision of, 50-51
World Wide Web
  color graphics cost, 52
  databases on, 113
  impact on CD-ROM multimedia, 28
  Infonautics' Electric Library, 118
  library access to, 50
  Library of Congress collections on, 99
  printers' and publishers' Home Pages on, 119-120
  vendors' Home Pages on, 107,109
Wright State University, 60
Wulf, William A., 5,10-11

Yankee (book vendor), 115

Z39.50 protocols, 121-122,124

For Product Safety Concerns and Information please contact our EU
representative GPSR@taylorandfrancis.com
Taylor & Francis Verlag GmbH, Kaufingerstraße 24, 80331 München, Germany

www.ingramcontent.com/pod-product-compliance
Lightning Source LLC
Chambersburg PA
CBHW052130300426

44116CB00010B/1848